Praise for *Remember Who You Are*

~~~~~

"Practicing the habit of loving myself and remembering who I am is amazing. **My awareness has shifted and I am able to stay in a positive vibration most of the time.** It feels so good! You're onto something valuable for us all!"

~ Cassandra Kostuk, USA

~~~~~

"These daily messages have generated great conversation between my husband and me! **This is helping us both grow together as individuals and as a married couple of 36 years!** Thank you for such wonderful work and sharing this in so many communities!"

~ Holly Hallet, USA

~~~~~

"I have been alone the last weeks and realize you are totally right - I was lost but now I know I need to be alone by myself to know myself."

~ Nate Hansford, USA

~~~~~

"I have had a breakthrough of sorts. In my mirror work, I was reminding myself of how far I've come, from a high school dropout to an almost published author, and all the garbage I've dragged myself through to get here, **and I realized that I'm my own hero!**"

"I began to cry! For about 5 minutes or maybe more...I wasn't keeping track. **All I know is that I had a real shift, and I haven't felt the same since!** Awesome!!!"

"This has made a difference in my self-confidence. When I spoke to myself this morning **I felt a shift and I really saw my soul!** And I thanked her! It was a wonderful experience I hope others can have as well."

~ Betty Horn, USA

~~~~~

"**I'm really connecting with my true self I think.** I don't know what it is...maybe I have shifted. I'm in a happy place. BREAKTHROUGHS!!!!!"

~ Debra Jones Hoffman

~~~~~

"Your messages are a true God send. **I am finally in a spot where I can recognize and find my true self and my energy and be happy.** "

"My six children and I are staying at the woman/child shelter now. Because of your emails I am doing well and staying strong in the shelter tonight after my husband strangled me and almost killed me."

"Without your help and your daily messages I don't think I would have been able to leave. **You have changed my life so dramatically the last few months. I am amazed at how strong I am becoming.**"

~ April Hanson, USA

~~~~~

"**Thanks for helping me to love myself, for reminding me who I truly am**, and what an opportunity we have to live a Truly Amazing Life and to keep our thoughts heading in the right direction."

~ Paul Posseno, USA

~~~~~

"I love your style of writing. It's encouraging, lifting, fun, and knowledgeable. I love having the audio. **I love that each day is only about 5 minutes**. And I love feeling a part of the TAL Family."

~ Leona Murdy, United Kingdom

~~~~~

"It took me most of the month to see this make any difference to me, until last night. **I stood at a mic on a stage and for the first time, was not scared.** I thought, "I can do this!" I opened my mouth and everything flowed freely and beautifully, it was one of the most pleasurable times I've ever had singing. So once again thanks man you've done me proud, and I am truly grateful."

~ Alison Mc guinness, United Kingdom

~~~~~

"**Connecting with myself daily has given me my confidence back that has been missing for a long time.** I trust myself again and know if I listen to myself, I have the right answers for me. It's OK to be just the way I am. Thank you!"

~ Kathy Eisnaugle, USA

Download The Audiobook Free!

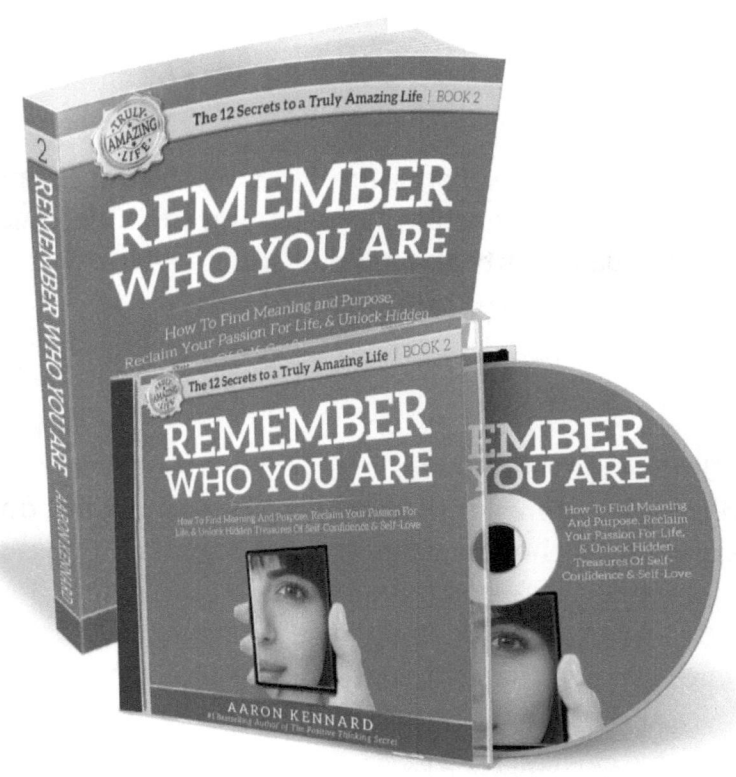

READ THIS FIRST

Just to say thank you for downloading this book, I would like to give you the Audiobook version 100% FREE!

Go to http://trulyamazinglife.com/rwya-audio

REMEMBER
WHO YOU ARE

*How To Find Meaning and Purpose,
Reclaim Your Passion For Life, & Unlock Hidden
Treasures of Self-Confidence & Self-Love*

AARON KENNARD

Published in the United States of America by:
Truly Amazing Life, Inc.
Website: www.trulyamazinglife.com
Email: support@trulyamazinglife.com

Copyright © 2015 by Aaron Kennard
All rights reserved.

Contents

INTRODUCTION

A Proven Path To Amazingness In Your Life 1

The Best Way To Read This Book 6

Additional Help & Resources 11

The 12 Secrets to a Truly Amazing Life - A Brief History 14

One More Tip and One Essential Tool 20

DAILY MESSAGES

Day 1 - Connect deeply with the real You - starting today. 25

Day 2 - Time to wake up and free yourself from the negative programming of the world. 31

Day 3 - The fastest pathway out of oppressive misery is directly inward. 37

Day 4 - We don't accidentally stumble into an amazing life. We must fully commit to it. 41

Day 5 - Be a wise master of the mansion of your soul. Refuse occupancy to the negative. 47

Day 6 - How to block out the noise and listen to your inner voice. 51

Day 8 - If you truly loved yourself, how would you act right now? 57

Day 9 - Practice avoiding comparisons that breed damaging lies. 63

Day 10 - Return to the deep waters of inner peace and confidence. 69

Day 11 - Compassion is the goal. It is the doorway to grace. 75

Day 12 - Discover the power of your eyes. 81

Day 13 - Yep, it hurts to dig into wounds. Do it anyway! 85

Day 15 - Some ways to enhance the conversation with your self. 91

Day 16 - There is a deep well of loving water within you. 95

Day 17 - All people are truly amazing, but many do not remember that yet.. 101

Day 18 - "Your job is purely to love yourself. Truly and deeply."..105

Day 19 - The importance of fierce, focused practice. 109

Day 20 - Crystal clear thoughts laced with joy..........113

Day 22 - The truth is you are OK just how you were created...119

Day 23 - A powerful story of the slow, painful grind of forgetting who we are.. 125

Day 24 - Securing the gold of the spirit...................... 129

Day 25 - Cherish each precious quiet moment you have with yourself!.. 135

Day 26 - "Our self-image and our habits tend to go together.".. 141

Day 27 - Life is magic when you truly believe in yourself.. 145

Day 29 - Bonus Day! One more thought to wrap up. 151

CONCLUSION

So What's Next? 155

What To Expect Going Forward 161

In Closing 163

How You Can Help! 165

A Proven Path to Amazingness In Your Life

Do you ever just feel disconnected from your self?

Do you crave a deeper connection with your inner soul?

Do you sometimes find it hard to look yourself in the eye and love what you see?

If so, this book has the power to produce a profound shift in your life.

This book contains a proven process to help you **find greater meaning and purpose, reclaim your passion for life, and increase your self-confidence & self-love** in the next 4 weeks or less, no matter your current circumstances...

...And it only takes about 10 minutes per day...including your time spent reading this book.

WELCOME TO: <u>Remember Who You Are!</u>

This transformational habit training system will restore your connection to your true inner self and transport you to a place of peace and power in your life.

Through 4 weeks of short, specifically crafted, inspiring daily messages, *you will be handed the key to unlocking the hidden treasures of increased self-confidence and self-love* that are ready and waiting inside you.

As you *Remember Who You Are* you will discover a deeper love and respect for yourself. This powerful love you will connect to affects all of your thoughts and actions in positive ways.

What you're about to experience has already improved hundreds of people's lives with its simple, systematic, and doable approach.

Here are just three examples of what many people have experienced with this habit training system:

~~~~~

"Before this, I was not in control of my life. My life battery was low. **My outlook on life has changed. I have regained my joy for life.** By remembering who I am, speaking to myself has truly uplifted my spirits."

~ Tebogo Mhinga, South Africa

~~~~~

"I have noticed my view of myself isn't very high at all, and I don't love myself enough! **It's only through starting to remember who I am that I have started to find peace.**"

"I absolutely loved your daily nuggets of wisdom. **It was an amazing month for me learning more and more how to remember who I really am**, and I truly see how important and key this is! Thanks again for all your amazing work."

~ Joseph Michael, United Kingdom

~~~~~

"These daily messages have been transformational. **I have been so much happier and more positive.** On a scale of 1-10, I give this a 10! I'm not just being nice either."

"**This has had a huge impact on me**. These pillars we are working on seem to be having a healing effect. **I have a brighter hope for overcoming my PTSD** and being able to accomplish the things I've only been able to dream of before."

~ Crystal Tavenner, USA

~~~~~

<u>I promise you will experience increased self-*confidence, greater love for yourself, and incredible feelings of joy and fulfillment*</u> when you commit to following the daily system within these pages.

The steps are very simple, so please don't make this harder on yourself than it needs to be. The process is not complex and you already have everything you need to begin, so don't allow yourself any excuse to wait until tomorrow.

Decide to start right now!

You can read this intro, plus the entire first chapter, *and* take all of the actions I recommend within the next 20 minutes.

<u>Today is *your* day.</u> Right now is *your* time to *Remember Who You Are* and uncover a depth of purpose and passion for life that cannot be obtained in any other way.

The true YOU is in there, patiently waiting. I guarantee you're going to love who you find! Because inside you is a soul more amazing and beautiful than words can describe. I'm so excited for your personal reunion!

On the official Truly Amazing Life® Poster it says this for a very important reason: "*Remember who you are.*

Look into your eyes. You will shed tears of joy each time you realize."

As you connect with the true you inside, don't be afraid to let the tears roll. They may not come the first day, or the 15th, but I assure you as you stick with the process laid out for you, <u>one day tears will come and you will be overcome with joy.</u>

As you continue this habit we'll establish together, those tears of joy will likely come for you regularly, as they do for me nearly every day.

My job here is to remind you, motivate you, and teach you six days each week for the next four weeks.

What's your job?

<u>Just open the book each day, read the daily message, and take the small, simple action!</u>

But first, allow me to share some tools and a bit of background before we jump in to this transformational training together.

The Best Way to Read This Book

This book contains daily trainings 6 days per week for four weeks. Each day can be read in just 5 to 10 minutes and includes motivation and a reminder to take simple actions that turn into habits that will transform your life.

It's not the words in this training that will transform you — **it's your actions turned into habit that will transform your life.**

Your action is the critical factor.

This system is designed to motivate you toward simple action each and every day, long enough for a new habit to be established.

You'll get a rest day once each week so you can catch up on a day you may have missed or just focus on the simple actions we are working on. Every 7th day there is no message from me, *that is on purpose.*

There Are Two Ways To Approach This Training

I *highly* recommend the first way, but I know some eager beavers like me will opt for way #2 so I'm just going to address it here.

Way #1: Consume this book ONE CHAPTER PER DAY for the entire month and don't skip ahead.

Focus on the one brief message designed for today and then TAKE THE ACTIONS prescribed.

Way #2: Read the entire book in just a few hours. Get inspired and embed the entirety of the course into your subconscious at once.

Then go back and RE-read one chapter each day for the entire month as you TAKE THE ACTIONS prescribed.

Why do I recommend Way #1?

Because the entire key to your success with this system is to build a habit.

Consuming information doesn't build habits.

Reading a book will not change your habits or establish new habits. The only way to establish a habit is to take action repeatedly and consistently over a long period of time.

Just reading a book in a day or two will certainly inspire you — and could leave an enormous impression on you and change the way you view the world entirely.

This alone, could possibly change your beliefs enough to induce a new way of acting in the future, which could lead to transformational habit...*but it's not a sure-fire thing.*

The sure-fire, proven method of taking control and transforming your life in a systematic way — is to make a commitment to taking small, simple actions every day.

Over time these actions will form into powerful, transformative habits that work all on their own to produce amazing results in your life.

The challenge with reading the entire book all at once is that you stimulate your mind with new information, *without doing the work to apply the information.*

Our minds *crave* new information. So it's a completely natural desire for you to want to read the entire thing.

But it's MUCH more effective to give yourself little doses of 'new info' stimulation each day — *and use that to motivate you to take action consistently.*

When you go on an information 'binge' — it will likely lead to action for a few days or a week because you're motivated...

...But then you find yourself craving more information.

And then the information in this book is no longer 'new' so it doesn't fill that craving and you're likely to leave it on the shelf and find other 'new' information, which invites you to take completely different and unrelated action.

What's the problem with that you ask??

It seems harmless enough, you feel inspired by the other new information right? Yes, and that is fine...

...But now you are likely to forget about the action you were inspired to take last week!

And now you're off to the races applying new information, before actually acquiring a habit from the inspiring information from last week.

This is a huge challenge all of us passionate about improving ourselves face...whether we acknowledge it or not.

It's the challenge of our information age...*there's too much information and not enough consistent action!*

If we fall into this trap we risk becoming the person who is always learning yet rarely improving.

The person who knows a lot intellectually but really knows little because they have not established the habit of acting on the knowledge they have attained.

Leo Buscaglia, the amazing 'Dr. Love' was known to have said: **"To know and not to do, *is not to know."***

So please, do yourself the service of taking this course one day at a time, and <u>committing to yourself to take the actions I will invite you to take.</u>

Without your personal commitment, followed up with your personal action — this system is worth probably **100 TIMES LESS** to you than if you *allow it to spur you to action that creates habit.*

If you simply cannot resist the temptation to skip ahead in this book, believe me, I understand and empathize.

I don't know if I personally could resist reading ahead — I love devouring books and I often read or listen to 2 or 3 every week.

So if you're a knowledge-craving soul like me, I encourage you to hold yourself back in this case.

Let tomorrow take care of itself! Just read today's message — then TAKE TODAY'S ACTION!

The action portion of this system is probably 500 times more important than the words and instruction portion.

If you have moved on to the next day without taking the previous day's action —STOP! DO THE ACTION FIRST! Then read the next day's training.

And if you really just couldn't resist, then make sure you don't sell yourself short...keep the commitment to <u>RE-</u>

READ each day's training when the appropriate day arrives, and take each day's action.

Additional Help & Resources

If you want to ensure that you don't forget to read the daily message, here's another very powerful option for you:

I will personally deliver each day's message directly to your email inbox at the same time each day, and I will read it to you in video and audio format, in addition to sending you the text to read.

Many people have found it extremely helpful to have me showing up each morning in their email inbox to remind them and keep them on track.

To take advantage of this daily reminder system, go to http://trulyamazinglife.com/rwya-bonuses.

Because of the cost of creation, hosting, customer service, and support required to maintain that system, in the past there has been a charge for that additional level of support and help. But that is my extra gift to you for purchasing this book.

I want to make sure that I am helping you establish these habits in every possible way I can.

So I am pulling out all the stops!

Joining the daily email delivery system is by far the most effective way this system has worked for people in the past.

It's not required of course...you can get the exact same benefit from this program by guiding yourself through this book each day.

And as mentioned on the first page — you can also download the full audio mp3's of this training for free and guide yourself through the audio each day if you prefer that format.

Just go to http://trulyamazinglife.com/rwya-bonuses

The great thing about what you've got in your hands right now is that you have a permanent reference in one place with all the guidance and inspiration this system provides you.

The most powerful combination is certainly using the daily email to remind you AND having the permanent record in the form of this book to refer back to.

By getting the daily email you'll be reminded to read the training each day. It is so crucial that you are consistent each day so that you establish a new habit.

Also, with the email you can *watch the video* and *listen to the message* from me while you read it which engages more of your senses and emotions and drives the impact of the powerful words much deeper.

So to take advantage of the daily email method of this habit development system, type this into any web browser:

http://trulyamazinglife.com/rwya-bonuses

The 12 Secrets to a Truly Amazing Life - A Brief History

The course you are about to embark on for the next 30 days is part two of a 12-month training series designed to help you live the 12 Habits of a Truly Amazing Life.

Standing alone this system can be transformational. When combined with the rest of the series it has proven to be incredibly life enhancing.

Here's some background information to get you up to speed:

This is the poster that started the Truly Amazing Life movement and shows the 12 pillars, or principles, that the 12 habits are based on:

(Go to **http://TrulyAmazingLife.com/rwya-bonuses** to download and print the poster for free)

That poster was created in the spring of 2012 after months of soul searching and many hours of writing as I asked myself the question *"Why is life so amazing?"*

At the time I was experiencing what can best be described as a euphoric six-month high on life. Not drug-induced, but joy-induced. Each day I was feeling completely blown away at the beauty of life, and I felt deeply compelled to capture why I was feeling such profound joy.

The result was that poster — summing up the principles that were creating so much joy and making me comment consistently to myself *"This Is A Truly Amazing Life!"*

After creating that poster and seeing it so clearly, it became my mission in life to make these 12 pillars of a Truly Amazing Life accessible, attainable, and simple for anyone to live worldwide...because I felt a calling from deep within to share the experience of joy I felt & still feel in living them each day.

Over the next couple years, I began to dissect those pillars and uncover the habits underneath each one. I discovered more than one habit relating to each of the 12 pillars, but I chose to focus on the one most fundamental and universal habit associated with each pillar for now...

...And that's where this book series comes in.

Over the course of about three years and thousands of hours of personal application and feedback from hundreds and hundreds of students testing these principles, a proven system and method has been created for establishing each one of the 12 fundamental habits as a permanent part of your life.

Each system is being published as a book in this series in order to allow as many people as possible worldwide to apply these transformational habits in their life.

Once the series is fully published in English, the plan is to then have it translated and published in many other languages.

These foundational 12 habits have become known as 'The 12 Habits of a Truly Amazing Life,' and they are shown on the Make Today Amazing poster here — created in 2014.

(Go to **http://TrulyAmazingLife.com/rwya-bonuses** to download and print the poster for free)

I encourage you to print and frame these posters and place them in your environment. It's an excellent way to help embed these essential pillars and habits into your life.

Having these posters printed will also be a wonderful visual reminder each day for you to take the actions I will be inviting you to take.

And to make it more clear — here's the big picture of the 12 Pillars, the 12 Habits, and the corresponding book created for each one:

	The Pillar	The Habit	The Book
1	Believe	Affirm	Affirm Your Truth
2	Remember	Reflect	Remember Who You Are
3	Smile	Appreciate	Smile! Feel Good Now
4	Enjoy	Move	Move Your Body
5	Think	Meditate	Think Better Thoughts
6	Succeed	Focus	Succeed Right Now
7	Give	Serve	Give Yourself Away
8	Create	Write	Create Your Life
9	Celebrate	Play	Play Every Day
10	Love	Forgive	Love Unconditionally
11	Grow	Read	Expand Your Mind
12	Empower	Listen	Empower Other People

One More Tip and One Essential Tool

Be patient and trust the daily process.

Over the course of this month we will be focused on the 2nd pillar of a Truly Amazing Life® — REMEMBER. The habit is to *reflect* each day in the mirror and *Remember Who You Are*.

Why is this habit so important?

Because unless you continually *Remember Who You Are*, you will drift away from fulfillment and inner peace, regardless of how good things are going externally.

Start the journey today by taking the first step. Don't worry about the remaining pillars and all the other wonderful things to learn and do.

You have all the time in the world. In fact, all you have is time, and *you are exactly where you are supposed to be right now*.

Trust that.

Whatever you experienced in the past has led you perfectly to this moment in time which was perfectly prepared just for you to experience.

So focus! *Make today amazing* with what you have right in front of you.

I can't wait to hear from you!

Please email me any time and let me know how you're progressing or tell me any challenges you are facing.

My email address is aaron@trulyamazinglife.com and I read every email that comes through.

While I'm not able to respond right away to every email, I do respond when I can, and I definitely read them all.

I love hearing from you!   Don't hesitate to reach out to me.

The One Essential Tool

Finally, here is an important tool I use every single day to stay on track. It will be extremely valuable for you:

The Truly Amazing Morning Weekly Tracker

The Truly Amazing Morning™

#	The Pillar	The Habit	Mon	Tues	Wed	Thu	Fri	Sat	Sun
1.	THINK	Meditate							
2.	SMILE	Appreciate Through Deep Gratitude							
3.	BELIEVE	Affirm The Truth & Envision Your Life							
4.	REMEMBER & LOVE	Reflect Love & Forgiveness To Yourself In The Mirror							
5.	GROW	Read Uplifting, Empowering Words							
6.	CREATE	Write What Flows From Your Heart							
7.	SUCCEED	Write Your Priorities for Today							
8.	ENJOY	Move Your Body Vigorously							
9.	ENJOY	Enjoy a Healthy Breakfast							
10.	EMPOWER	Truly Listen & Genuinely Compliment Someone							
11.	GIVE	Do A Selfless Act Of Service For Someone							
12.	CELEBRATE	PLAY! (Sing, Dance, Laugh, etc.)							
	Time of Day of Self Check-in								
	How Do You FEEL? (Write 3-4 short words or statements)								

Week Ending _____

© 2014 – TrulyAmazingLife.com — Feel Free To Share With People You Love ☺

(Go to **http://TrulyAmazingLife.com/rwya-bonuses** to download and print the tracking sheet for free)

This tool is a weekly accountability tracking sheet containing all 12 habits of a Truly Amazing Life®. I keep a stack of these printed and each week I place a fresh one at the front of my journal. I begin every day with this checklist.

It keeps me on track and helps me focus on the highest priorities first every day.

It's a guide and reminder of the specific habits of nourishing and connecting with your own soul each day.

In order to live a Truly Amazing Life you've got to *Make Today Amazing.* If you don't focus on making *today* amazing and you consistently wait until tomorrow to live fully, then you simply won't live a truly amazing life.

<u>The best way to ensure that you Make Today Amazing is by starting the day with a Truly Amazing Morning Routine.</u>

We are only focused on the 4th habit on that list this month. But at least some of the others you are most likely already doing. Keep those up if you're in the habit!

But don't let yourself be distracted trying to establish more than one habit at a time. Focus on establishing just this one habit this month: **Remember Who You Are**.

Each of the other books in this series will go into great detail on the other habits...all in good time. I encourage you to begin to implement this tool in your life.

Okay, the groundwork has been laid and you now have everything you need to succeed with the pillar of 'Remember' this month.

Let's jump right in to day one!

Day 1 - Connect deeply with the real You - starting today.

It's time to *Remember Who You Are*!

I'm so excited to work on this incredibly important pillar with you this month.

For the next four weeks, I will be inviting you to focus on the habit of reflecting in the mirror in order to *Remember Who You Are.*

Some may think, "How can I remember who I am if I have never known who I am?"

The You with a capital Y knows and has always known who you are.

Each day, whether it's the first time or the 1000th time, when you become aware of who you are it will likely feel more like a *remembering* and a *welcome home* than a new discovery.

It is an important distinction that you are 'remembering' and not 'discovering,' because in truth this is not a new discovery. Who you are is well known to your True Self and it is simply up to you to remember what You already know.

The knowledge of who you are is inside you.

A daily process of remembering is essential. Just because you remember today, doesn't mean you're all set, and your work is done.

Tomorrow is a new day. When you wake up tomorrow, today will not exist anymore. You will be a new person, with new experiences, and new challenges.

Remembering who we are is an important daily practice for the rest of our lives in order live to our highest potential.

Life, peers, the Jones family's many possessions and their seemingly perfect life, our ego, and all the other influences around us constantly pull us in so many different directions.

It is our job to maintain a remembrance of who we truly are constantly, in order to hold firm and steadfast in our resolve and purpose.

Living on purpose is essential to a Truly Amazing Life.

When we forget who we are and we forget our purpose, we drift.

When we drift, our thoughts and emotions lead us down undesirable paths of boredom, lethargy, pessimism, anxiety, and eventually despair.

However, when we know with crystal clarity, who we are, why we are here, and where we are going, our life is filled with *energy* and *light*.

We are deeply happy within ourselves.

We find meaning and joy in every outside circumstance, whether it is the painful trudging through harsh storms, or the peaceful walks on sandy beaches.

When we remember who we are, we know that we are enough.

We need nothing outside of our self.

We are at peace.

And we are powerfully humble and happy.

So with that, here is your small and simple task for the next four weeks in order to establish the daily habit to *Remember Who You Are*:

REFLECT

Each day, first thing in the morning, and sometime before bed, follow this simple 4-step process:

1. **Sit or stand directly in front of a mirror.** (Get close, within a foot or two.)

2. **Breathe in and out deeply 3 times while looking in your eyes.**

3. **As you look in your eyes say this 3 times:** "(Say your name), I forgive you for every mistake of the past. I love you fully and completely. You are worthy. You are capable. You are amazing. (Feel free to add other truths about the real You)."

4. **Breathe in and out deeply 3 more times.** (Still looking in your eyes.)

Do this process twice per day, every single day for the next four weeks.

If you miss a day, don't worry; I'll be here to remind you each day. Simply get back on track and do it the next day.

You don't have to be perfect to establish a habit. *Just do your best.* The more consistent you are the better of course.

As you do this 4-step process morning and night for four weeks with sincerity, I promise you will notice a shift take place in your heart.

It's very possible you will have monumental shifts and breakthroughs in happiness and peace like you've never experienced before.

If you have never done this practice before, it is likely to bring you into a relationship of love with yourself that you have never known. <u>You are likely to feel like you made a major discovery of the real You.</u>

In reality, it will be a remembrance. Because *You* know who *You* are, *you* just forget...sometimes for a long time. *You* have been there all along waiting patiently for *you* to slow down and notice.

For some, the shifts may be subtle. You may find that you become just a little more compassionate, a little happier, or a little more grounded.

<u>But you will notice a shift.</u>

So go forth! Start the habit of reflecting *You* back to yourself twice today!

I'll be back tomorrow with more encouragement and insight.

Make today amazing!

Day 2 - Time to wake up and free yourself from the negative programming of the world.

How did it go yesterday?

Did you do the four steps in the morning and the evening?

Here are the four steps again:

1. **Sit or stand directly in front of a mirror**. (Get close, within a foot or two.)

2. **Breathe in and out deeply 3 times while looking in your eyes.**

3. **As you look in your eyes say this 3 times:** "(Say your name), I forgive you for every mistake of the past. I love you fully and completely. You are worthy. You are capable. You are amazing. (Feel free to add other truths about the real You)."

4. **Breathe in and out deeply 3 more times**. (Still looking in your eyes.)

And here are the four steps simplified:

1. Look in the mirror
2. Breathe
3. Say 'I love you' 3 times
4. Breathe

Easy. Do that every morning and every night this month. If it's hard to look in your eyes, <u>do it anyway.</u>

Don't be surprised if you get emotional and begin crying. **That is good**.

Also don't worry if you aren't getting emotional right away and you feel no impact. **You are having an impact!** <u>Doing this process twice a day is impacting you whether you feel anything or not.</u>

Try to keep yourself open to exploring your heart as you do this each day. At some point, sooner or later, you will shed tears of joy as you *Remember Who You Are* deep within your core.

Now...why are we doing this?

Isn't this a bit weird to talk to ourselves in the mirror?

Sure...maybe it is a bit weird. But the better question is this:

How badly do you want to tap into the deep reservoir of personal confidence, love, and power that dwells within you?

That is why we are doing this.

You will get over any feelings of awkwardness in time, and you will feel the sense of peace and confidence that you deeply yearn for.

By expressing your love for yourself daily for four weeks you will establish the habit of believing that you love yourself and actually feeling that love on a deep, subconscious level.

Your self-image and self-worth will improve dramatically.

And that is essential to your happiness and the achievement of your goals and deepest desires in life.

That internal love for yourself needs to be such a core part of you that it automatically guides your outlook and thoughts at all times. And that will happen as you diligently follow the process each day this month.

I'll leave you with an important truth today:

You are *more* than worthy of love.

Unfortunately, it is extremely common for us silly humans to believe the exact opposite.

We sometimes feel guilty and unworthy of love from others and ourselves.

We attach our self-worth to our accomplishments or possessions or a myriad of other things outside of ourselves — which inevitably leads us to the pain of unwarranted self-criticism.

David R. Hawkins gave us a marvelous insight on this in his book *Letting Go: the pathway to surrender*:

"When we look deep within ourselves, <u>is it not because of our very innocence that we believe ourselves to be guilty?</u>"

"It is because of our own inner innocence that we have bought into all the negativity of the world and allowed it to kill our aliveness, destroy our awareness of who we really are, and <u>sell us the pathetic little smallness for which we have settled.</u> Is not ours the innocence of the newborn that cannot defend itself and, with no capacity for discernment, could only allow itself to be programmed, like a computer?"

"To see this means to become conscious."

"Let's wake up and free ourselves from being exploited and enslaved by the negative programming of the world."

"When we see the truth of how programming happens, we will see that we are the pure, blank computer."

"We are the innocent space in which the programming is occurring."

"<u>Once we have looked deep within ourselves</u> and found that innate inner innocence, we will stop hating ourselves. <u>We will stop condemning ourselves and stop buying into the condemnation of others and their subtle attempts to invalidate our worth as human beings.</u>" - David Hawkins

The computer of your mind has been programmed by negative influences throughout your life...and that's OK! Because you can delete those programs by remembering now who you truly are.

<u>Remember...you are *more* than worthy of love from yourself.</u>

One final idea: It's important to track your progress with this habit.

I recommend using the Truly Amazing Morning weekly tracking sheet and making a check mark every time you keep this daily reflection commitment to yourself.

Download the tracking sheet at:

http://trulyamazinglife.com/rwya-bonuses

Draw a diagonal line through each day's box on the Remember line (line 4) so that you can make a check mark for the morning and a check mark for the evening.

Keep a record of each day you keep the commitment to reflect love for yourself in the mirror.

It feels good to see the progress you are making and it also holds you accountable to yourself.

You are much more likely to have breakthrough results if you keep track of your progress and hold yourself accountable.

Now go remember how awesome you are!

Make today amazing!

Day 3 - The fastest pathway out of oppressive misery is directly inward.

How are you doing using the mirror to reflect love to yourself at least twice each day?

If you are struggling, join the conversation in the TAL Mastermind community and ask for help.

Go to http://trulyamazinglife.com/tal-mastermind

If you are having breakthroughs, share those and let us celebrate those wins with you. This will also encourage others who may be struggling.

We are here for each other.

We are much more alike than we tend to realize. So don't be afraid to share openly. In the TAL Family there is loving support for everyone in the ups and the downs.

Don't sell yourself short by trying to be an island of independence. Come join the community.

Now, *why* are we doing this again?

Here's one reason…

"**The misery that oppresses you lies not in your profession but in yourself!** What man in the world would not find his situation intolerable if he chooses a craft, an art, indeed any form of life, **without experiencing an inner calling?**"

"Whoever is born with a talent or to a talent, must surely find in that the most pleasing of occupations! <u>Everything on this earth has its difficult sides!</u> Only some inner drive — pleasure, love — can help us overcome obstacles, prepare a path, and lift us out of the narrow circle in which others tread out their anguished, miserable existences." - Johann Wolfgang Von Goethe

Why should we connect to ourselves and discover what our heart calls to us?

Happiness.

<u>True happiness only comes from within us.</u> That's the simple fact of the matter.

Yet we are constantly pulled by the world to seek happiness outside of ourselves.

"Only some inner drive — pleasure, love," says Johann, can "lift us out of the narrow circle in which others tread out their anguished, miserable existences."

What we are doing here is purposely seeking to know ourselves and to love ourselves deeply.

As you make a sincere effort multiple times every day to reconnect with You — your soul, your spirit, your heart — you will grow a deep love for yourself.

You will come to know yourself more clearly.

You will begin to discover your heart's passion and calling.

Because you are actively listening to your heart, instead of hushing it through escapism, repression, suppression, or projection of your emotions.

This may take time. It may even take months or years.

But it is so critical to your lasting happiness in life to have the habit of deeply connecting with yourself regularly — every single day is best.

By establishing this habit to *Remember Who You Are*, you are putting yourself on the path of happiness, fulfillment, growth, mastery, and enlightenment.

Without this habit of deep connection with yourself — you will veer.

We all do.

Even though I teach this stuff and I'm immersed in the 12 pillars of a Truly Amazing Life® every day, I also have daily need to reconnect with Me.

Nobody is exempt from the need to nourish their most fundamental relationship.

If I don't do it, I start veering off-track pretty fast. It's human nature to get distracted by the world.

We overcome our "natural man" by establishing healthy habits.

This habit is so important.

I'm eager and excited for you to get it! I want to hear about your experiences, your insights, and your transformations as you come to know and love yourself more deeply this month. So make sure to share in the TAL Mastermind.

Keep it up! You can do it.

Remember Who You Are.

Make today amazing!

Day 4 - We don't accidentally stumble into an amazing life. We must fully commit to it.

Hello! Today I will introduce you to my friend Kamal Ravikant.

You may know him if you've read his books, *Love Yourself Like Your Life Depends On It* or *Live Your Truth*.

He has written some powerful words of wisdom for you on this immensely important topic.

His life was changed overnight after he hit the rock bottom of depression and hopelessness when **he suddenly became fully aware that he had the freedom to choose to start loving himself.**

He quite literally began a constant affirmation to himself right then that he kept up all day, throughout the day: "I love myself."

It revolutionized his life.

And now it is revolutionizing hundreds of thousands of lives because he has shared his experience in two powerful books that have sold all over the world.

I encourage you to add the simple statement '**I love myself'** into your thoughts throughout the day and let it lift you all day long.

Do that in addition to the time spent in the morning and night in front of the mirror.

Just start saying 'I love myself' over and over and over again.

It will greatly help you in this process of falling deeply in love with the amazing person you are.

That's what Kamal did and he became immensely happy. He began living the Truly Amazing Life of his birthright.

But it required his *total* commitment to himself.

He says:

"One thing I've learned: **we don't stumble accidentally into an amazing life."**

"It takes decision, a commitment to consistently work on ourselves. The best ones I know, they do it daily. A focused

<u>practice.</u> *They fail, but they pick themselves up, continue forward. If there is any secret, that is it.* **Over time, the days blend into a life that amazes the world**." - Kamal Ravikant

That is so true.

And the fact that you are diligently pursuing this habit through this program shows that you have the commitment, and have decided to work on yourself.

I know you can establish this daily practice of loving yourself. I know you can make the deep commitment to yourself to forgive yourself and to get back on the horse every day no matter what.

Here's another powerful question from Kamal for those times when we are feeling beaten up by life, or by our own emotions and negative thought patterns:

"If I loved myself truly and deeply, would I let myself experience this?"

If we are feeling bad about ourselves, the answer is, "NO! Of course not!!"

Well…we can change it.

We can start right now by saying, "I'm sorry self! Please forgive me. Thank you! I love you. I love myself!"

We can forgive ourselves and be happier right now.

How long are we required to wallow in self-pity and misery and self-loathing?

Is there some magic time limit we are required to suffer? One day? A month? Or is there a two-year requirement of suffering before we can choose to forgive and love ourselves again?

Of course not!

We can forgive and love ourselves right now!

So why do we not forgive ourselves sometimes?

<u>Because we feel unworthy of love.</u>

A final thought today from Kamal:

"The truth is to love yourself with the same intensity you would use to pull yourself up if you were hanging off a cliff with your fingers." - Kamal Ravikant

The truth is this: <u>YOUR LIFE IS ON THE LINE!</u>

Your happiness this day is on the line! This is a critical situation. There's no more time to sleepwalk through life, numb yourself and forget about the inner emptiness.

This very moment, if you are not loving yourself completely and fully, you are not living the full potential of your amazing life.

But you can!

You can start now.

Let's do this together today. I love you. I see the real You…the one yearning to live in love and light. *Remember Who You Are.*

Make the commitment right now that you will forgive yourself, and love yourself deeply. Love must start within you, for you.

That commitment is essential to living a Truly Amazing Life®.

Make today amazing!

Day 5 - Be a wise master of the mansion of your soul. Refuse occupancy to the negative.

Hello again! Did you love yourself yesterday?

Did you repeat, "I love myself," throughout the day in addition to your time in the mirror morning and night?

Good! Keep it up!

If you struggle to remember, or get distracted by your usual habits of thinking, **don't worry!** And don't beat yourself up.

That's why I'm here for you again right now.

It's OK. We all fall off the horse. Just be kind to yourself. Say, "It's OK. I'm OK. I'm getting back on today and I love myself!"

Then go forth and do your best. Recommit to You right now.

There's a good reason why this is a daily process. **A day is a long time!**

One day is our whole life in one sense. We only experience life today. We don't live tomorrow and we don't live yesterday.

We only live right now!

That's why it is *vitally important* to establish the daily habits of living a Truly Amazing Life®.

We don't live life 'this week' either by the way. This week is future, and we don't experience our lives in the future.

We need to establish the habits of living in pure joy, love and truth every single day.

The amazingly inspired author James Allen wrote something that underscores why we are telling ourselves "I love myself."

This is why we are filling up our heads with that thought:

"*He who would be useful, strong, and happy must cease to be a passive receptacle for the negative, beggarly, and impure streams of thought;*"

"*As a wise householder commands his servants and invites his guests,* **so must he learn to command his desires and to say, with authority, what thoughts he shall admit into the mansion of his soul.**" - James Allen

I love the imagery of not allowing the negative, unworthy impurities to enter into 'the mansions of our soul'.

Instead, we consciously choose loving thoughts to abide there, and we fill our soul with those thoughts.

We leave no vacancy, and no room at the inn, for the negative thoughts that are beating at the door.

Thoughts of unworthiness, incapability, inferiority, fear, weakness are not allowed.

And the only way to keep those negative thoughts out is to fill our minds up to the brim with loving, truthful thoughts.

You are lovable. You are worthy. You are capable. You are strong and courageous.

Don't believe otherwise, because the opposite of that is a lie that will only fill you with false fear and and bring you down.

Keep repeating, "I love myself!"

If you don't feel like you love yourself, then say that statement as a command to yourself to start loving yourself!

Refuse to accept unloving behavior toward yourself.

And keep connecting with You daily in the mirror, at least morning and night.

Here's a reminder of the 4 simple steps:

1. 1. **Sit or stand directly in front of a mirror.** (Get close, within a foot or two.)
2. 2. **Breathe in and out deeply 3 times while looking in your eyes.**
3. 3. **As you look in your eyes say this 3 times:** "(Say your name), I forgive you for every mistake of the past. I love you fully and completely. You are worthy. You are capable. You are amazing. (Feel free to add other truths about the real You)."
4. 4. **Breathe in and out deeply 3 more times.** (Still looking in your eyes.)

Remember Who You Are!

Make today amazing.

Day 6 - How to block out the noise and listen to your inner voice.

Have you ever noticed yourself silencing your inner voice?

Perhaps not, because it mostly happens without our conscious awareness. But there's a part of each of us that tries to *forget* who we really are.

Because if we forget, then we can justify doing things we would not do otherwise.

As if by forgetting it releases us from the need to treat ourselves with loving kindness and truly respect our own soul.

Regarding this, the Spanish philosopher Jose' Ortega Y Gasset in the early 1900's said this:

"**Among his various possible beings each man always finds one which is his genuine and authentic being**. The voice which calls him to that authentic being is what we call 'vocation.'"

"*But the majority of men devote themselves to silencing that voice of the vocation and refusing to hear it*. They manage to make a noise within themselves...to distract their own attention in order not to hear it; and *they defraud themselves by substituting for their genuine selves a false course of life.*" - Jose' Ortega Y Gasset

Part of our goal this month is to ensure that we do NOT follow the course of the majority of men and women Jose' was referring to!

Our aim is to listen to and follow our authentic inner voice.

By choosing consciously to love ourselves each day, to look into our eyes and connect deeply, to listen to what our soul has to say, and to feel it deeply,...

...It's like we are building up a secure fortress around our mind and heart each day that will block out the noise of distraction and lies that bombard us.

Remember the mansion from yesterday?

As you *Remember Who You Are* each day it's like closing the gate and locking out the imposters who would otherwise come in screaming and shouting throughout the halls of your mind!

As you keep your inner refuge calm and silent you will be able to hear the voice of your soul that calls you.

You can only follow your heart if you can hear your heart.

If we don't spend the time reconnecting daily, we inevitably turn to escaping from ourselves or looking for something to distract our attention from the inner void of disconnection.

We must confront the truth of who we are daily and put the ego, that smallness and falseness inside us, where it belongs...

...In the back seat, or in the trunk, or out the window where it cannot keep driving our life.

We confront the truth daily when we say, "I love myself!"

This will be painful to the ego, which hates us, and to its lies which we have previously allowed residency in our hearts.

You know...those lies of, "You're not worthy", "You're nobody special", "You can't do it", "You're not as good as them", and every other similar falsehood.

Those lies don't want to leave!

They have set up a cozy camp and they're comfortable right where they are. And they will likely make a big fuss on their way out the door.

We all have disempowering beliefs that have been camping out for a while inside, and it usually hurts to uproot them and give them the boot.

In fact, I would not be surprised if they are putting up some resistance inside you right now just hearing themselves being called out.

But oh the liberation you'll feel as the truth sets you free!

The truth being this: "<u>You are amazing, worthy, and capable of deep joy, happiness, love, and greatness. I love you!</u>"

That truth will set you free.

Speak that truth to yourself often.

Treat yourself with complete and total love today. Do the small simple thing of connecting in the mirror morning and night. Tell yourself, "I love myself," throughout the day.

Do that and you will *Remember Who You Are*.

Tomorrow there is no message from me — that's by design.

A one-day break from the routine gives you a clear division between each week of disciplined focus and lets you recharge your energy.

While you're taking a break from my daily messages, I also encourage you to take a full day break from your other regular distractions…

…Like TV, news, social media, email, etc.

When we shut out the noise and chatter of the world we can hear the beautiful things our heart has to say more clearly.

Doing this intentionally each week is a very valuable practice in itself.

But do continue with the practice of reflecting love to yourself in the mirror tomorrow.

I'll be back in two days with a lot more insights to share on this incredibly important topic.

Make Today Amazing!

Day 8 - If you truly loved yourself, how would you act right now?

Welcome to week 2 of *Remember Who You Are!*

How do you feel?

Are you feeling the truth of how amazing you are?

Are you seeing your powerful, deeply loving soul more clearly?

If so, that's great! Keep going deeper each day into yourself.

Your soul is deep, and the practice of deep connection with yourself can grow more profound throughout your life.

If not, that's OK too!

Don't give up. Stick with the practice.

Remember, "By small and simple things are great things brought to pass."

It's very common not to notice changes that are happening to us as they happen. A lot of change is imperceptible because it happens slowly over time.

<u>Think of this like you're building a house out of bricks.</u>

Every time you say, "I love myself," you are laying down a brick. And every time you look in your eyes and say, "I forgive you and I love you completely," you are spreading some mortar to connect those bricks.

You can't always see much progress as you're laying the bricks, but every little thing you do in a positive direction is helping.

<u>Trust the process.</u>

Do the action to create the habit morning and night even if you don't feel amazing.

When you step back and observe at some point you'll see how all those little daily actions have stacked up and created something beautiful.

After about a month you will have a habit that is yours to keep.

There is immense power in owning positive habits.

With a habit, before you realize it a year has passed, and you've been connecting with yourself and loving yourself consistently for an entire year. You will then see clearly that great things have happened in your life and heart as a result.

In all likelihood you will see results much sooner, but be patient. <u>Do the process faithfully.</u>

Now, a few more words of wisdom from an inspired individual:

"If you make friends with yourself you will never be alone." - Maxwell Maltz

Why is it that so often we find ourselves trying to escape from ourselves?

We do it in so many different ways.

Here's a tip for you: When you notice yourself taking your favorite habitual escape route, use that as a reminder to love yourself.

For example, if I am procrastinating something hard, like writing this book, a typical escape route is to walk into the kitchen and eat something. Or to check in on a myriad of distractions on my computer.

Think about your common escape routes for a moment. What do you tend to do to avoid difficult things or procrastinate?

Next time you notice yourself doing your typical escape route, stop and say:

"If I truly loved myself would I do this thing right now? No. I love myself. I love myself. I love myself."

I've found when I start slipping into 'escape mode' due to overwhelm or other negative emotions, it's hard for me to want to look in the mirror.

A good practice is to make this decision and commitment to yourself:

"When it's hard to look in the mirror, that means I must do it."

When I feel like escaping, one of the best things I can do for myself is go to the nearest mirror, look into my eyes, and start a dialogue like this:

"How do you feel? How do you want to feel?"

"I love you. You are awesome. Do you really want to do this or are you escaping some negative feelings?"

"I forgive you for whatever you may have done to contribute to this negative feeling."

"I love you. You rock. I believe in you and your greatness."

"I forgive you for your weaknesses and love you anyway."

Make friends with yourself!

Be kind to yourself.

In addition to repeating, "I love myself," it's a wonderful thing to get real with yourself throughout the day and check in often.

I keep a big mirror right by my desk for this very purpose.

If I start feeling down at all, I sit back, and take a long, deep breath. Then I look over and remind myself how awesome I am and that life is truly amazing.

I start feeling grateful.

It shifts my emotions to a more positive place very quickly.

It's an amazing thing to be in a loving relationship with your own self. When you treat yourself as a loving friend, you can always have a loving companion.

That companionship with your own powerful, loving, amazing soul, will replenish your storage tanks of inner confidence, purpose, and peace.

Remember Who You Are. Love yourself.

Make today amazing! :)

Day 9 - Practice avoiding comparisons that breed damaging lies.

Here's a powerful truth from Maxwell Maltz in his book *Psycho-Cybernetics*:

"Within you, whoever you may be, <u>regardless of how big a failure you may think yourself to be</u>, is the ability and the power to do whatever you need to do to be happy and successful."

"<u>This power becomes available to you just as soon as you can change your beliefs</u>. Just as quickly as you can de-hypnotize yourself from the ideas of "I can't," "I'm not worthy," "I don't deserve it" and other self-limiting ideas."

You are absolutely amazing and you have the power within you to do things you can't even imagine right now.

We all do!

But what's the key to unlocking the power within that leads us to freedom, fulfillment, joy, and so many other amazing emotions?

The key is to *"de-hypnotize yourself from the ideas of "I can't", "I'm not worthy", "I don't deserve it", and other self-limiting ideas."*

And you can do that! You are doing that!

De-hypnotizing yourself from the lies that have been programmed into the operating system of your mind and heart is not complicated.

It's exactly what we are doing together right now; we're re-programming our inner machine through this process of daily repetition.

Each day we are installing empowering truth, one small thought at a time.

But it's a conscious thought and a purposeful process. We are *choosing* to believe something better.

One moment at a time.

One day at a time.

Every time we repeat our truth we strengthen the neural pathway in our brain that carries that belief.

This is the process of de-hypnotizing yourself from subconscious beliefs that you may not even realize are there.

You totally deserve immense happiness.

You are completely worthy of deep feelings of love.

You are absolutely capable of accomplishing amazing things in the world.

Remind yourself of all of that in the mirror.

As you repeat the truth that you are worthy, loved, and capable of amazing things, don't be surprised if it brings discomfort.

If those positive, loving thoughts make you feel uncomfortable that is evidence that you are hypnotized by at least some lies that are not serving you.

Reject any lies you feel inside that say you are not worthy, not capable, not good enough, not lovable, and not amazing.

Choose to give forgiveness and love to yourself instead. Choose to believe the truth that you are amazing.

Believe me, I get it. I get bombarded all the time by lies that try to destroy my peace.

They usually come the moment we start comparing ourselves to others.

So let's stop comparing ourselves OK?

I know that is a monumental challenge for many of us...but each step we take to avoid judgment and comparison makes it just a little bit easier to avoid comparison the next time.

We increase our non-judgment ability with practice just like everything else. And the skill of non-judgment frees us from a whole host of lies that don't serve us.

Mike Dooley who writes a popular daily email called *Notes From The Universe* said this about comparisons:

"Comparisons are odious because they assume all other things are equal which is rarely the case."

And when it comes to us compared to others, it's never the case!

We are each totally unique. So it's complete silliness to compare ourselves to others.

Yet we tend to get sucked into it. So just be aware. And go back to the truth.

What truth?

"I love myself. I forgive myself. I am OK. I am unique and amazing."

Keep repeating the truth, in the mirror, and you will de-hypnotize yourself from the false and limiting beliefs.

Remember Who You Are!

Remember to check in with yourself morning and night. Don't leave yourself hanging! A loving relationship requires nurturing.

Be there for yourself today!

Finally, here's one quick addition to the mirror technique that will enhance your ability to connect and get emotional: **Write to yourself.**

If you are finding it challenging to connect to yourself deeply, try this combination:

First look at yourself in the mirror and follow the 4 simple steps, speaking out loud. Then pull out a journal and start a dialogue with yourself on paper.

Just start by writing the things you have been speaking:

"I forgive you for every mistake of the past. I love you fully and completely. You are worthy. You are capable. You are amazing."

Then let the conversation go wherever it feels right. I recommend writing as many other sincere compliments to yourself as possible.

This combination of speaking and writing can be *extremely* powerful.

For some who have struggled to feel a deep connection through conversation in the mirror, writing has proven very effective at bridging that gap and eliciting powerful emotion.

Our focus this month is to *Remember Who You Are* and connect you to You daily. Whatever helps you best do that each day is all that matters in the end.

Make today amazing!

Day 10 - Return to the deep waters of inner peace and confidence.

Good job sticking with me! You're moving right along in this empowering process of improving your relationship with YOU.

Keep it up. You are doing great!

And if you just said to yourself, "Hey, no I'm not. I've been slacking and it's been challenging to keep my commitment to reflect to myself every morning and night," ...

...That's OK!

You are still doing great! Why??

Because you are reading or listening to Day 10 of this system.

That means you are still here, still making some effort, and you can start again right now.

If you have been slacking, I'll just ask what Tony Robbins likes to ask, "When is now a good time to start again?"

Life happens now. Yesterday is done. Tomorrow doesn't exist. There is only right now.

And you are OK right now.

If you have experienced challenges remembering who you are, or beating yourself up, or anything, remember to ask for help! You don't need to go this alone.

Come join the Truly Amazing Life® Mastermind community and speak up!

Go to http://trulyamazinglife.com/tal-mastermind

If you are experiencing breakthroughs, don't deny others the blessing of celebrating those with you!

Share your success with those who will celebrate it with you. If the family or friends around you don't understand, you can be sure your Truly Amazing Life® family gets it.

We're a family of people who understand each other. We can celebrate the highs with you and we can handle the lowest of lows. So feel free to share and don't hesitate to ask for help.

We are all attacked by lies and negativity.

Don't think for a minute that you are alone when you experience the discouraging feelings of unworthiness, incapability, or unhappiness.

Every person who is being honest will acknowledge feeling those feelings. It is part of life and progression to get bombarded by oppression from negative thought.

Nobody is free from the influence of negative thought in this world.

Negative thinking generally brings feelings of shame, so it's not easy to speak up when we are being bombarded by negativity.

We feel weak, we feel inadequate.

We get easily convinced we are flawed because the lies of negativity crowd the space in our heads, leaving little room for the truth.

But You are not your thoughts!

And the true You is far from unworthy or incapable.

Just know that you are understood. And nothing you have done or can do makes you unlovable. Especially in the TAL Family, we all get it. We are here to support each other.

So remember that, and come support others as well.

And now, a couple powerful truths from David Hawkins:

"The end result of the conscious handling of emotions is <u>invulnerability</u> and <u>imperturbability</u>. Our inner nature is now bulletproof. <u>We are able to go through life with balance and grace</u>."

He also said...

"<u>With this increased awareness of who we really are comes the progressive invulnerability to pain.</u>" - David Hawkins

In other words, as you *Remember Who You Are*, you become progressively bulletproof inside.

Less and less hurt or moved by pain.

Less and less able to be upset.

Imagine yourself as a deepwater fish in a large, deep lake. The rough tumbling rivers (the negativity, worries, and problems of the world) flow into the lake and get absorbed and calmed in the vast stillness of its flat waters.

No outer circumstances disturb you.

Even heavy winds have no affect below the surface where all is confidence and peace.

You can come to live in a state so peaceful and confident within yourself that all hell can break loose around you and you are completely 'imperturbable'. (Or the made-up word I prefer, unbuggable!)

This is because you know who you are and why you are here, and you are living in a state of deep love, compassion, and understanding.

Have you had those days, when you felt nothing could get you down?

By establishing this constant, deep connection to who you truly are, *you can live in a state of confidence and peace every single day.*

Maybe up until now you have been the deepwater fish in a river. Sometimes you come to a deep pool in a flat valley where all is peace and you feel unstoppable.

But swimming on the next day you suddenly find yourself tossed back and forth out of control in agitated waters again.

That's what happens when you forget who you are.

You are a deepwater fish!

<u>Remember Who You Are</u> and return to the deep water.

Your inner confidence, peace, and happiness will then see you through all the inevitable challenges of life with grace.

You will live free of the suffering caused by worry over the future.

Keep up the daily practice in the mirror! Breathe. Look deep into your eyes. Express love, forgiveness, and confidence in yourself.

Make today amazing!

Day 11 - Compassion is the goal. It is the doorway to grace.

Welcome to another stunning day of life!

You are alive! Did you stop to ponder on how awesome that is yet today!?

This Is A Truly Amazing Life.

The fact that you woke up and air filled your lungs, your body is functioning, and your brain is running all your systems flawlessly, is a miracle. It's amazing!

The fact that you are able to read or listen to this message from across the world from any digital device is also amazing.

Think about how miraculous today's technology would have seemed hundreds of years ago.

I just want to remind you first today to soak in the beauty of the fact that you are alive on this planet and blessed with a physical body.

Even if your body is in pain you can be grateful...

...Because deep pain enables deep joy.

And now, another thought on who you really are from the inspired David R. Hawkins:

"The only way to enhance one's power in the world is by increasing one's integrity, understanding, and capacity for compassion."

"Compassion is the doorway to grace, <u>to the final realization of who we are and why we're here</u>, and to the ultimate source of all existence." - David R. Hawkins

COMPASSION!

Truly, what matters more than compassion?

When you gain a feeling of compassion for yourself, it accompanies forgiveness and a feeling of deep reverence and awe at the miracle that you are.

When you feel that, the door opens to reveal who you are and why you are here.

Compassion opens the door to insight and revelation straight from the source of your creation, because the energy of compassion and love is what you were created from.

Hawkins said compassion is the "doorway to the ultimate source of all existence."

I want to go through that door!

So I do. :) Every day if possible.

And why do you suppose it feels so good to feel compassion for someone? Or to feel forgiven? Or to feel forgiving?

Because that is the energy of the true You!

That is the energy of your creation, and when you are connected to it you can feel your soul singing with joy.

It feels amazing.

Pause for a moment. Look in your eyes and say this: "I love you. I forgive you, because I see *You*. I see your inherent innocence and desire for goodness, and I forgive you for all of the things you perceive as weaknesses. I see the real You."

How does that feel?

That is compassion. Pass it on to yourself! Seriously.

That's the doorway to the final realization of who you are and why you are here.

You were created of compassionate love; it's in every fiber of your being.

And just because negative programming and false beliefs have been loaded into your mind and heart since you were young, and they give you feelings of unworthiness sometimes, ...

...<u>That doesn't change the truth of who you are</u>.

Express love, gratitude, and kindness to yourself and you will remember who you truly are.

And that changes the entire course of everything.

Your life, and your action, and everything flows with grace when you are connected to the real You.

It no longer feels like a heavy, impossible burden to do good, and to be productive, and to accomplish amazing things.

It feels natural.

Life is still challenging, but it's a fresh, invigorating challenge that accompanies compassionate purpose.

Remember to connect to the real You today in deep compassion.

Here are the simple steps again:

1. **Sit or stand directly in front of a mirror**. (Get close, within a foot or two.)
2. **Breathe in and out deeply 3 times while looking in your eyes.**
3. **As you look in your eyes say this 3 times:** "(Say your name), I forgive you for every mistake of the past. I love you fully and completely. You are worthy. You are capable. You are amazing. (Feel free to add other truths about the real You)."
4. **Breathe in and out deeply 3 more times**. (Still looking in your eyes.)

Go ahead and add conversation and questions to yourself in that process.

The point is to connect deeply to You daily. However you do that is wonderful. Those four steps are simply a guide, but really, when you look in your eyes and see yourself, words are not even necessary for deep connection.

It may even be hard to put your feelings into words.

Just be you. Be real. Focus on the goal of compassion and connection.

Make Today Amazing

Day 12 - Discover the power of your eyes.

Today you will hear from the man who taught me the mirror technique, Claude Bristol.

He wrote about it in *The Magic Of Believing* in 1948. That book is amazing and packed with truths relating to many of the 12 pillars of a Truly Amazing Life®.

Here's what he said regarding the mirror technique:

"Much has been written about the power of the eyes. The eyes are said to be the windows of the soul; they reveal your thoughts. They express you far more than you imagine. They permit others to "get your number," as the saying goes."

*"**However, you will find that once you start this mirror practice your eyes will take on a power that you never realized you could develop**; this power will give you that penetrating gaze that causes others to think you are looking into their very souls."* - Claude Bristol

I have modified Claude's suggested mirror technique in our practice to include statements of love for yourself.

He recommends standing up straight, breathing in deeply 3-4 times, and then telling yourself in your eyes exactly what you want most.

What is your vision for your life, or your desire for this day? He suggests telling yourself that you are going to get it; that you will make it happen.

For example, I would look into my eyes and say, "I'm going to finish writing this book this week."

For whatever is important to you, <u>if you commit to yourself in the mirror, looking in your eyes, it adds power to your commitment</u>.

Feel free to add some of your commitments to yourself in your morning and evening mirror practice.

Just tell yourself what you want and that you are committed to making it a reality. It has a powerful effect.

But the most important thing is to *Remember Who You Are!* So don't stop that practice for anything.

Here's another thought on the compassion topic from yesterday:

"Once we compassionately accept our own humanness and that of others, we are no longer subject to humiliation, for true humility is a part of greatness." - David Hawkins

Does this mean that we will never again experience humiliation?

It doesn't for me. Because I don't always stay connected to compassion.

But each moment that we compassionately accept our humanness and that of others…in that moment we are free.

Free from humiliation because we are truly humble in that moment.

But what about 5 minutes from now? Or an hour?

How about tomorrow? Are we still in that place of complete compassionate acceptance of ourselves and others?

The reality is the cares of the world will be back to bombard us daily; judgment, comparisons, jealousy, etc. We are not free once and for all from all negative thought and influence just because we were free once.

That is why the daily practice to *Remember Who You Are* is so essential.

And once per day is not even enough, especially at first when you are reprogramming a lot of negative mental junk that has built up over years.

That's why you need to reconnect in the mirror at *minimum* morning and night.

Claude Bristol also had this to say:

"To win you've got to stay in the game." - Claude Bristol

Life is a game that is won or lost every single day.

You don't just play and win one day and then you're set for a while.

You've got to engage consciously with life every day in order to live the *Truly Amazing Life* of your birthright.

What we are doing together is creating the habits that get us showing up fully in life as a natural tendency.

Then life becomes magic...especially when you compound all 12 habits of a Truly Amazing Life on top of each other.

Be diligent in your practice today! *Remember Who You Are* in the mirror at least morning and night.

Make today amazing!

Day 13 - Yep, it hurts to dig into wounds. Do it anyway!

Wow, we're already near the end of week 2! I'm so glad to be on this journey with you!

Thank you for your commitment to this practice. I applaud you for your desire to deepen your connection to your true self daily.

I believe it is one of the most important and valuable things you can do for yourself and others. I'm grateful for you.

Here's another thought from Claude Bristol to follow up from yesterday:

"*Every person is the creation of himself, the image of his own thinking and believing.* **As individuals think and believe, so they are.**"

Every single time you think, "I love myself," you create that as a deeper reality. You combat those lies of "I'm not worthy," and, "I can't do it," that make you feel like hating yourself.

You are the creation of yourself.

You get to choose what thoughts you will entertain.

If you are busy thinking empowering truths, guess what? *There's no room left for the false and limiting beliefs to rear their ugly heads.*

When you have a song stuck in your head that you are sick of...how do you get rid of that endless loop?

You just turn on a song that you like!

The two songs won't fit together at the same time in your mind.

It's the same principle here. By *barraging* ourselves with, "I love myself," throughout the day we leave no room for self-degradation.

That's also one of the great reasons to repeat the affirmations of truth we began with in book one of this series: "Everything is conspiring for my benefit," and, "This is a truly amazing life."

Any and all empowering, positive truths you can actively program your mind with will do the job of keeping negativity out and creating beauty in your life.

Your mind is your tool to wield and control.

You are the master...not those random wandering thoughts.

I truly hope you are connecting to your *true self* each day.

I hope you are finding it easier each day to look deep in your eyes and see *the majesty*, *the beauty*, and *the power* within you.

I hope you are overcome with humility and gratitude for what you see, and the gift of life you have been given.

I want to hear from you. How is it going? Send me an email at aaron@trulyamazinglife.com and let me know.

Share in the Truly Amazing Life® Mastermind community.

Go to http://trulyamazinglife.com/tal-mastermind.

As the TAL Family, when we collectively share our truths, and the experiences we are having, it expands the consciousness and awareness of those around us.

We are all better for that.

One real possibility I recognize though, is that you may be struggling still to look in your eyes and see beauty.

You may be heavily weighed down with either guilt, sorrow, or shame, somewhere deep inside, which makes it very difficult to look in your eyes and say, "I love you," and actually mean it.

You may not even know why you feel this way.

This practice could very well have exposed some deep, dark feelings that you have unconsciously suppressed for many years.

Please don't give up if that's what is happening for you!

That is a very good thing actually!

It is extremely common actually for people who begin this practice, to struggle severely with it at first. Some have shared that they break down in tears the minute they look in their eyes and have to look away.

If that's you, please don't give up! This is so important for you.

You are uncovering deep wounds that have been buried and festering for a long time.

And those wounds will continue to infect your life with sadness, misery, and suffering in different ways until you heal them with the truth.

It hurts to dig into wounds, so we all naturally turn away from doing it.

Be strong! You can do this. Know that you are on the right path, and *DO IT ANYWAY*.

If it hurts to look in your own eyes...*DO IT ANYWAY!* That's when you need *You* most!

<u>You are on the path to freedom.</u>

I love you. You are worthy. Despite what the ego and the false programming in your head may tell you, **you are amazing.**

And you are going to see that very clearly at some point, probably soon. And you will shed tears of joy when you do!

You'll get a break from my messages tomorrow. I'll be back in two days.

Keep up your habits!

Reflect morning and night! Don't let up now...you are almost half-way. Commit to being diligent for the rest of the month.

And be compassionate to yourself and all others when you fail.

Be kind, merciful, and forgiving. That is the way to true happiness.

Make today amazing!

Day 15 - Some ways to enhance the conversation with your self.

Welcome to week three on the journey to *Remember Who You Are!*

Today we'll start with a quote from my short book *The A to Z of a Truly Amazing Life*:

"Y is for You"

"Remember who you are. Look into your eyes. **You will shed tears of joy** each time you realize."

"There is power and joy in remembering who you are and it is essential to true happiness. Forgetting this always brings unhappiness."

"But you can always remind yourself."

"Just look in the mirror and ask, "Who are you?""

"Allow answers to flow and keep asking until you feel the complete joy of knowing that you are an infinite, joyful, powerful, loving, and creative being!"

"Ironically forgetting yourself by serving others is the other sure-fire way of reconnecting to the real you."

And now today let's talk about two enhancements to our mirror practice you can add to the mix this week.

Keep doing what you've been doing of course: "I love you" in the mirror at least twice per day & repeat the phrase "I love myself" throughout the day.

But now, enhancement 1: Feel free to mix in more discussion in the mirror (if you haven't already).

Loving and forgiving and accepting yourself are the keys.

Adding more real discussion with yourself can greatly facilitate that. As mentioned in the quote, feel free to ask yourself, "Who are you?" **And listen for the answer!**

Ask whatever questions are on your mind…**but ask them to your self, looking in your eyes.**

Here are some great things I like to hear directly from myself:

What do you want most?

What makes you deeply happy?

What makes life so amazing to you?

Who are you?

What are your greatest strengths?

What do you love doing more than anything else?

Why do you love that so much?

Think about it, if you were dating someone, wouldn't these type of questions be great ways to get to know that person deeply?

So do it for yourself! You need to know yourself deeply. **You need to Remember Who You Are**.

So I invite you to enhance the conversation with yourself this week.

And here's enhancement 2: this comes from a technique that one TAL Family member Leona M. shared:

"Having had a stressful morning where my self confidence dipped, I have had to force myself to look in the mirror and use a technique along side Aaron's to bring myself back to me and to feel calm and peaceful again."

"Basically, I took my name and for each letter of it I replaced it with a word that reminded me of my true self."

"So I said, I am Leona, I am…."

- *Loving*
- *Enthusiastic*

- *Open minded*
- *Natural*
- *Amazing*

"This is what I say most days but because today was harder I wanted to use strengthening words so I added a new one,"

- *Lioness*
- *Energy*
- *Optimistic*
- *Nerve*
- *Accepting*

What do you think? Feel free to give that a shot if you need an extra boost.

It's week three. We've established the daily habit now and its roots will go deeper this week.

Let's go even deeper into our soul along with those roots. Let's get to know ourselves even better.

Let's dive deep and remember what our soul has been whispering to us our whole lives but sometimes we've forgotten or we've kept it too noisy to hear.

Make today amazing!

Day 16 - There is a deep well of loving water within you.

How did it go asking questions of yourself yesterday?

Keep doing that. Allow yourself to remember deeply who you are by asking yourself specific questions and listening for the answers.

This is best done in the quiet, early hours of the morning for me.

But whenever you have quiet, peaceful time is a great time to reconnect with You.

Now, a question for you today:

Have you ever thought, "What is wrong with me?"

Welcome to the club! Everyone has thought that at one time or another.

I got this heartfelt, vulnerable email from a TAL Family member Wendi one day that you may be able to relate with:

"My biggest challenge is even though I have just about everything I could possibly want in life, I'm still not happy."

"I want to be happy, I'm just not and I don't know why. I put on a fake smile for everyone around me in hopes they won't notice how unhappy I truly am."

"I find life in general to be a challenge...when I think back on a time I was happiest...I was living alone in an awesome townhouse in a different state than my parents. I had an awesome job, I worked out at the gym everyday with a friend, and I was within driving distance from the beach, which is my happy place. The only responsibility I had was myself. I am not a selfish person, I enjoy helping others and taking care of my kids."

"So what is wrong with me?"

Ever felt like Wendi? I definitely have.

I remember one time when I was feeling low I was playing on the trampoline in the perfect shade of a warm sunny evening, looking up at the peaceful clouds, and my three girls were all giggling hysterically. I distinctly remember thinking that the circumstances warranted only feelings of unbridled joy...and yet I could not feel joy. I felt empty. I smiled at the kids, but it too was empty for me.

I wanted to feel the joy, but in that moment I couldn't for some reason...just like Wendi.

Here are my thoughts on that:

Happiness is a choice.

Getting everything you want will never bring you true & lasting happiness.

There is definitely nothing wrong with us if we find ourselves struggling to be happy.

In those moments we just need to be guided back to remembering which choices to make.

Here's the guidance:

If you actively live the 12 Pillars of a Truly Amazing Life, *happiness is inevitable.*

It's simply unavoidable. Happiness and joy are the natural outcomes of living those pillars.

And the pillars are all *actions*, as you'll notice when you look at the Truly Amazing Life Poster.

Living the 12 pillars of a Truly Amazing Life allows you to live in a state of joy regardless of your circumstances. To have that level of control over your state of happiness and joy requires that your happiness come from within.

That is why we are so focused this month on the essential pillar of *Remember!*

Remembering who you are is absolutely critical to finding deep and lasting happiness within.

As you noticed above, *Wendi had been looking for happiness outside of herself.* We *all* fall into this; it is the nature of the physical world and society we live in to pull us into looking for happiness in external things.

Remember what she said?

"Even though I have just about everything I could possibly want in life, I'm still not happy. I want to be happy, I'm just not and I don't know why."

There's a very simple reason why, and we would all do well to remind ourselves of this daily...

<u>TRUE HAPPINESS IS ONLY FOUND WITHIN.</u>

As long as we look for happiness in things around us, achievements, possessions, relationships — ANYTHING outside of ourselves — we will be disappointed. True happiness will never be found.

It really is as simple as going within, and being aware that <u>nothing</u> outside us can or will produce true happiness and we will always be frustrated if we try to make things do that.

So go within today. Just like you have been doing daily for over two weeks now.

Remember Who You Are.

Uncover that deep love that you have for yourself that has been stifled to some degree.

There is a deep well of love within you.

Dig down to it. Drink deeply from the pure, crystal waters of that love.

Inside you is a spring that is ever flowing and never dries up, and it will constantly fill you and quench your thirst for happiness.

And once you are filled with that living water of joy and happiness that springs only from within, you radiate a powerful energy of love to all around you and encourage them to dig down to their own well of pure happiness and loving, living water within. You don't have to even try, the energy of joy and love naturally radiates out from you, embeds itself in all you say and do, and positively impacts everyone around you.

You rock. You are amazing. You can do this.

Keep doing this simple habit daily — **Remember Who You Are.**

Make today amazing my friend!

Day 17 - All people are truly amazing, but many do not remember that yet.

Hello again! Congratulations on being alive on the planet for another day of this amazing life!

I like being alive...in fact I daresay I love it. I hope you are loving it too!

Let's talk about freedom for a minute or two...starting with another quote from *The A to Z of a Truly Amazing Life:*

"Freedom"

"I do not believe we came to earth to discover the secrets to a 'pretty good' existence."

"It's not compatible with our true nature, to waste even one moment settling for a second-rate, miserable experience in any aspect of our lives."

"By choosing to complain and settle we bind ourselves in mediocrity."

"Each person on earth is equally endowed with freedom to choose to live in awe and gratitude."

"All people are truly amazing, but many do not remember that yet so they move about in denial of their chains of quiet misery, sacrificing their precious gift of life."

And why do they not remember they are truly amazing?

There are many reasons.

But the bottom line is we've all been fed a **bunch of lies** about who we are from a **bunch of sources** for a **bunch of years**.

And we have unwittingly consumed those lies, installed them as beliefs in our subconscious, and re-fed them to ourselves over and over.

The lies of unworthiness, incapability, being undeserving of love, and the biggie, **"I'm not good enough."**

But now we are feeding ourselves the truth. Purposefully. Daily. Keep doing that!

Keep telling yourself the truth. "I love myself. I am amazing. I am perfectly capable. I am immensely powerful." And on, and on, and on.

<u>You are truly amazing and your life is truly amazing.</u>

Anyone who tries to convince you otherwise is blind to who you truly are.

I SEE YOU!

I know who you are.

Because you come from the same source I come from.

I know your true nature. It is the nature of pure, loving compassion for all of life and creation.

If you plant the seed of those words in your heart and watch as they produce the fruit of peace and joy and happiness within, you will know for yourself they are true.

It has been well said, "By their fruits you shall know them." You will know that is true you by the way it makes you feel.

Now we'll finish today by returning to our topic from yesterday with a powerful statement from David Hawkins about where true happiness is found:

"<u>Out of the recognition of who we really are comes the desire to seek that which is uplifting</u>. When that inner emptiness, due to lack of self-worth, is replaced by true self-love, self-respect and esteem, we no longer have to seek it in

the world, <u>for that source of happiness is within ourselves.</u>"
- David Hawkins

This is far and away the overriding theme of the pillar of *Remember*.

I have met and talked with people who are living most of the pillars of a Truly Amazing Life, but because they are missing this essential pillar, *they do not know who they are and they are depressed!*

I have a friend who is incredibly successful in business and he is really good at motivating others toward business success. But he is lacking this inner awareness of who he is and so he continues to struggle with depression.

Remembering who you are today, and every day of your life, is of the most vital importance.

It cannot be overemphasized.

Go now, do your practice, keep on reminding yourself who you are.

Make today amazing!

Day 18 - "Your job is purely to love yourself. Truly and deeply."

Today I want to share one TAL Family member's experience with this habit of remembering:

"Because of your program I might actually be able to save my marriage, which was in a huge state of distress, <u>most or all due to the lack of belief and faith in myself.</u>"

"I've always valued my life, but **I have never really known how to be truly happy within myself**. As I grew into a young mother trying to find my way with no guidance it was hard but God helped me through it."

"<u>But I was just getting through it. I settled for an OK life</u>. Mostly because it was all I've ever known. But now I'm never going to settle for anything less than an amazing life"
- April H.

How was it possible for her to stop settling and start living a truly amazing life?

Largely because she remembered who she truly is.

She recognized that the lack of belief and faith in herself was causing her distress.

April discovered how to be truly happy within herself by remembering who she truly is.

If you have discovered that for the first time, or the 1000th time, through this process of remembering that we are working on together, that is awesome! Re-discovering that is the goal...every day of your life.

Keep going every day. Allow this habit to *Remember Who You Are* be firmly embedded in you.

Life contains challenges that you cannot foresee.

Staying in the habit of remembering who you are enables you to meet those challenges with grace, to overcome them all, and to experience joy and fulfillment throughout the process.

When we forget who we are, we flounder. We feel lost, and confused. And sooner or later we sink into boredom, settling, despair, or all the way to depression.

A Truly Amazing Life is built on small, simple, habitual ways of thinking and being.

So keep building this habit.

You are deep into it now, and this habit can and will serve you for the rest of your life when you establish it and keep it.

Here's another powerful quote from Kamal Ravikant from *Love Yourself Like Your Life Depends On It*:

"*Your job is purely to love yourself. Truly and deeply. Feel it. Again and again.* **Make it your single-minded focus.** *The mind and body will respond automatically. They don't have a choice.*" - Kamal Ravikant

I love how he separates your mind and body from YOU!

YOU have the choice...not your mind and body. YOU are the master.

The reason I love how he said to make this your 'single-minded focus' is because it takes HUGE effort and DISCIPLINED focus in the beginning to get the momentum of a new habitual way of thinking and being.

You won't always have to focus so intently on loving yourself.

In time it will become your nature to automatically love yourself and remember who you are. With practice you will easily reflect and speak love and kindness to yourself morning, evening, and all day long.

But in the beginning, single-minded focus on this habit is so important.

Getting a new habit to replace an old one is a lot like getting a big boulder rolling down an incline. If you do it half-heartedly, you'll never get it rolling.

It requires a lot of focused effort at first, getting it rolling a little faster, then a little faster. If you keep at it long enough it becomes easy to keep it rolling. Eventually the habit takes over like gravity and keeps the boulder rolling on its own.

So keep focused!

Forgive yourself if you faltered a couple days.

Get back up and keep going. **Focus on today**! Reflect love to yourself morning and evening at minimum.

You are amazing.

Remember Who You Are.

Make today amazing!

Day 19 - The importance of fierce, focused practice.

Hello again! I'm so excited that you are well on your way to the firm creation of the habit to Remember Who You Are.

I've got a couple more nuggets for you from Kamal Ravikant today from his powerful book Love Yourself Like Your Life Depends On it.

"I think instead of reading loads of self-help books, attending various seminars, listening to different preachers, we should just pick one thing. Something that feels true for us. **Then practice it fiercely.** Place our bet on it, then go all out. That's where magic happens. **Where life blows away our expectations**." - Kamal Ravikant

Kamal makes a very good point here.

Certainly he's not advocating avoiding positivity from many sources. Of course we want to surround ourselves with positive influences as much as possible.

I think he's pointing out that there are a lot of people who teach a lot of different things that probably work great *if you actually DO them.*

But when you try to do too many things, your focus is spread thin, and you do none of them well, if at all.

That's exactly why together we spend an entire month focusing all our energy on creating one habit at a time.

Habit creation requires focused, fierce practice.

Complete dedication to **just one thing.**

And the beauty of that is when we do completely dedicate ourselves to one thing, **life is so simple!**

FOCUS removes overwhelm and gives us a sense of calm.

Once we establish a new habit firmly, it doesn't require the same amount of energy to keep it going. We can maintain many good habits, but it's best to fiercely focus on establishing just one new habit at a time.

Keep your eye on the one goal this month — to Remember Who You Are every day.

Reflect in the mirror morning and night.

Repeat throughout the day, "I love myself."

Practice this fiercely, with laser-like focus for the entire month.

Keep tracking your progress! Check off the days so that you can hold yourself accountable and see your accomplishments.

Here's another statement to try adding to your talks in the mirror. If you say this to yourself while standing tall, there's no way you won't be empowered and uplifted:

"This day, I vow to myself to love myself, to treat myself as someone I love truly, deeply. In my thoughts, my actions, the choices I make, the experiences I have, each moment I am conscious, **I make the decision I LOVE MYSELF.**" - Kamal Ravikant

Feel free to add that to your morning mirror routine.

In fact, printing that out and posting it next to your mirror is not a bad idea.

Or you can write statements like that with dry-erase marker right on the top of your mirror.

Do whatever it takes to love yourself fully today!

Make today amazing!

Day 20 - Crystal clear thoughts laced with joy.

Welcome to Day 20! It's a beautiful day to be alive!

First of all — **you are amazing**! I love you.

Thank you for being part of my life and allowing me to serve you. That's a gift you are giving me because serving, teaching, and lifting others is a huge source of fulfillment for me. So thank you!

Second of all — as we wrap up our 3rd week establishing the habit to *Remember Who You Are*...

...I want to talk about your calling.

What is your life's task?

What are the talents and attributes unique to you?

What is the gift only you can give while on this planet?

Robert Greene wrote a fantastic book in 2012 addressing this topic called *Mastery*. He shares some incredibly valuable insights and reminders:

"Some 2600 years ago the ancient Greek poet Pindar wrote, "**Become who you are by learning who you are.**"

"What he meant is the following: you are born with a particular makeup and tendencies that mark you as a piece of fate. It is who you are to the core."

"**Some people never become who they are; they stop trusting in themselves; they conform to the tastes of others, and they end up wearing a mask that hides their true nature.**"

"If you allow yourself to learn who you really are by paying attention to that voice and force within you, then you can become what you were fated to become — an individual, a Master." - Robert Greene

Many people begin noticing by now, after 19 days of focused inner connection, that they are starting to hear their inner voice more clearly.

I would not be surprised at all if your life's calling is becoming more clear to you throughout this process, without even having focused on that.

That's what happened to me, when I began this process of daily reflection and remembering…

…**I became aware of my heart calling to me.** As I heard that voice, that 'force within me,' it almost always brought forth tears of joy. (Don't worry, tears are not required. I may be extra emotional.)

I saw the real me.

As I kept my commitment to myself each day to connect deeply, and look in my eyes, new visions would open up. New feelings and new understandings.

I gained *clarity* and *confirmation* of who I am, and why I am here on this planet.

It was through this process that I became crystal clear that I am here to help others live a Truly Amazing Life.

That's who I am at the core. I am a lover of life and a servant.

I came to realize that my heart's primary purpose in life is to help others escape the bondage of mediocrity and suffering and fully live the truly amazing life of their birthright.

That awareness came through this mirror connecting habit we are establishing together right now.

<u>This process has brought me deep fulfillment, guidance, drive, energy, greater passion for life, and increased enthusiasm.</u>

This clarity of purpose has given me an immense amount of strength to overcome the obstacles that I face.

I would not be surprised if you are hearing your inner voice more clearly by now.

Don't worry if not though. In time you will as you persist.

I encourage you now to start listening closer this last week of this month, and on into the future, because within you is the source of your creation, all knowledge, and immense power.

Listening to your inner source will fill you with joy, clarity, and purpose.

Sometimes I hear my source through just feelings. <u>But most often it's crystal clear thoughts laced with joy that spring up in my heart and mind.</u>

Robert Greene adds this important nugget to the discussion:

"You possess a kind of inner force that seeks to guide you toward your life's task — what you are meant to accomplish in the time you have to live."

"In childhood this force was clear to you. It directed you toward activities and subjects that fit your natural inclinations, that sparked a curiosity that was deep and primal."

"In the intervening years, the force tends to fade in and out as you listen more to parents and peers, to the daily anxieties that wear away at you. **This can be the source of your unhappiness — your lack of connection to who you are and what makes you unique."**

"The first move toward mastery is always inward — **learning who you really are and reconnecting with that innate force."**

"Knowing it with clarity, you will find your way to the proper career path and everything else will fall into place. It is never too late to start this process." - Robert Greene, *Mastery*

I could not agree more with Robert on this. An inner disconnect is the source of unhappiness for so many people who I have seen and spoken with. It is also the main reason I ever find myself feeling unhappy.

When you do not remember who you are or why you are here, you seek happiness outside of yourself, which invariably perpetuates emptiness and unhappiness.

So keep on connecting deeply with *You* daily!

Tomorrow you'll get a break from my daily messages, but stay true to your daily practice.

Make today amazing!

Day 22 - The truth is you are OK just how you were created.

CONGRATULATIONS!!

If you have been diligent these past 21 days then you now have established the habit to reflect in the mirror daily and *Remember Who You Are!*

This habit alone will be responsible for deep happiness throughout your life.

Because when you are connected and in tune with who you are, then you can hear your calling in life.

You reside in a state of compassionate love, which spreads out and positively affects everyone around you.

And you are able to live in a place of *awareness*, *confidence*, and *deep fulfillment*.

So congrats for being at this very place at this time.

If life has handed you storms or you've struggled with distractions these past few weeks and you have found it challenging to establish this regular mirror check-in routine, *please don't beat yourself up inside!*

Acknowledge your responsibility in it. Don't pretend to be a victim of life. Just acknowledge what happened. Look at what lessons you can learn. *Then move ahead.*

You are OK. And you too are amazing. We are all at different places and there is zero benefit in judging ourselves or comparing ourselves to others.

It does not say anything negative about you or your character if this has been challenging for you.

What it says is you have experienced challenging circumstances. *That's all.*

Your heart is all that matters and your heart is in the right place. The proof of that is that you are reading or listening to this right now.

You are not in control of all things and we all have difficult loads to bear that come at different times.

Love yourself.

Forgive yourself.

Forgive life and God and everyone else around you for your challenges. Because in truth, all of these things are conspiring for your benefit, despite whether you can see how or not.

You are deeply loved and cared for, and you are completely deserving and worthy of immense love.

Your actions or lack of actions don't determine your lovability...

...*the fact is you are <u>always</u> unconditionally loved and cared for.*

Believe that.

Let go of self-judgment and condemnation — I guarantee you your creator is not condemning you.

We condemn ourselves by believing lies of negativity. We are all part of the same source of all truth, unconditional love, and compassion — not condemnation. Allow yourself to be free of any of the comparisons and the 'I'm not good enough' thoughts, which are completely false.

This too is part of remembering who you are.

Whenever you remember the truth and it resonates deeply in your core — you have remembered somewhat who you are — because you are connected to the source of all truth.

Now...let's wrap up today with a couple more thoughts from the inspired Kamal Ravikant:

"When your sense of self and happiness comes from within and isn't a roller coaster ride dependent on others or circumstances, you approach life differently. You make better choices. You draw to you the people and situations that matter. The others, they fall away."

And one more...

"**Peace is saying to yourself, "it's ok."** Peace is knowing that the maze the mind plays in is not the truth. Peace is knowing that life is. Just is. How we choose to react to it determines our reality." - Kamal Ravikant

Let go of any judgment today, whether positive or negative, and be at peace.

Both positive and negative judgments of yourself and others are rooted in ego and pride, which are always based in falsehood.

The truth is you are OK just how you were created!

Striving to be just like, or better than, any other person is a recipe for unhappiness.

Have a wonderful first day of the week!

Don't let up on your daily routine.

And as a reminder, hopefully you are in the habit of using the Truly Amazing Morning Tracker I gave you in the intro to this book.

Here's the link to the resources page where you can download it again if needed:

Go to http://trulyamazinglife.com/rwya-bonuses

This tool is indispensable for me. It keeps me on track and accountable to myself every day.

When creating habits and rituals it is extremely important to keep track of yourself using a check list.

It keeps your mind freer and more relaxed to have a simple list you can check off rather than needing to spend mental energy thinking about what to do next or trying to remember how you have been doing.

When it's black and white in ink in front of your face it brings you right into the present moment and reality instantly.

If I didn't have this list, I would more easily forget, and likely fall out of some of the core habits that are so beneficial to me.

Make today amazing!

Day 23 - A powerful story of the slow, painful grind of forgetting who we are.

Hello! It's a wonderful day to be alive. Thanks for being here…I'm so glad you are staying committed to this process.

Right in the middle of writing this book, I happened to do an interview with my friend Katie McCarthy and I was surprised and intrigued by the direction the call took.

I had literally just finished writing Day 13 and I was astonished at how perfect her experience related to what we have been working on together.

Here's the short version of her impactful story:

First, about a year prior, she went out on a limb in an act of amazing courage and faith, and quit her comfortable and prestigious corporate job. She struck out on her own as an entrepreneur, with absolutely no idea what she would do.

She simply knew she had to quit.

Her heart made that very clear, and *she followed her heart*.

Over the next year she went on to create an impactful podcast, interviewing successful entrepreneurs and sharing their wisdom, focusing on the deeply human and emotional aspects of being an entrepreneur.

But when the podcast didn't perform to her expectations in the first two weeks, she started comparing herself negatively to all the "more successful" people around her. Then she classified herself as a failure.

But she didn't even realize she had done that internally.

And the result became 6 months of grinding away at the work and losing touch with herself, her purpose, and her calling.

As we spoke, it was only two weeks after she had experienced a complete re-awakening and become aware that <u>she had forgotten who she was and what she was all about.</u>

She finally realized she had fallen into working for all the wrong reasons — reasons that didn't line up with her true self and her purpose.

When she made that discovery it completely set her free from the internal suffering and struggle. Here's what she said about it:

"<u>Once I got over this failure story, I started to acknowledge the actual gifts that I have.</u>"

"Before two weeks ago my concern and attention had been on how to have an impressive business, how to generate revenue. All the ego centered aspects of business — which is not why I became an entrepreneur. It had devolved into time, money, and looking good."

"When I was able to reconnect to who I am and the divinity of who we all are, I became aware of all these amazing things and people around me."

"And all of a sudden everything in my life was reframed in a positive way. **Everything instantly went from bleak and I'm not good enough, to MY LIFE IS AMAZING! Now I don't ever want to go to sleep anymore.**"

"I've always been the kind of person who seeks to learn a lot of things but <u>the place I always resisted looking for learning was inside myself</u>. Now I've started to ask my body what it wants. I'm asking myself questions, instead of asking other people for their opinion and guidance."

"And you know what? **I've been answering!!**"

"And that has been so profound. To know that the love that I was seeking outside of me, I have an infinite well-spring of that inside, and all I needed to do was look in the right direction."

As soon as Katie remembered who she is her life *instantly* shifted back to *truly amazing*.

The same will happen for you every single day you Remember Who You Are.

Life is truly amazing when you Remember Who You Are!

Let's follow Katie's example today and seek guidance and inspiration from the source of all knowledge and power within ourselves.

More on this tomorrow...but for now...

...Make today amazing!!!

Day 24 - Securing the gold of the spirit.

Today we're going to check in with a number of experts on the topic of remembering who you are.

"*If you are never alone you cannot know yourself.* **And if you do not know yourself you find fear of the void.**" - Paulo Coelho

I love that last statement.

It speaks so clearly to why we seek to escape the void through food, distraction (TV, Social media, email, etc.), alcohol, sleep, or even excessive exercise, friendship, sex — whatever our distraction of choice is!

And that's not to say those things are all bad for you...but they are commonly used as tools for distraction and comfort instead of being used in balance for prudent enjoyment.

We use physical things to escape from our own inner selves because we are afraid of the void we perceive

within in us — *which feels like an icy cloak over our entire life.*

It's a scary thing to confront! Nobody tends to want to confront big scary voids!

So we whip out our most trusty escape mechanism, which comforts us initially and leaves us feeling even worse and more afraid later.

<u>How do we stop this vicious escape/fear cycle?</u>

Simple: Be alone with yourself. Be quiet. Do the routine we are practicing this month. **Remember Who You Are.**

That's literally all there is to it.

Don't believe the internal lie that this needs to be hard. Just because you may have been running scared from the perceived inner void for a long time doesn't mean it has to be complex to stop.

You can just stop. <u>Stop running away and turn inward.</u>

And the next time you find yourself running from yourself (which happens to us all), just stop again. Look in the mirror. Look in your eyes and *Remember Who You Are.*

Here's another truth….

"One secures the gold of the spirit when he finds himself." - Claude Bristol

Not only do we remove the fear of the void, <u>but we secure the gold</u>!

Have you experienced that this month?

For me, that gold often comes in the form of healing tears, deep peace, and a feeling of profound love and mercy that feels like it's bubbling to the surface of my heart and spilling out.

I hope you have been securing that gold of the spirit this month. It is the most precious treasure in life and makes me want to hold onto this habit forever.

Here's another beauty...

"We must let go of the life we have planned, so as to accept the one that is waiting for us." - Joseph Campbell

We're so often making plans without consulting ourselves. Ludicrous I know! But we all do it.

Any time we get caught up and obsessed over what we *THINK* we want without being connected to what we *FEEL* from our true self, we tend to be fighting against our fate and against our heart's true calling.

You can tell this is happening when your heart is no longer singing and everything feels like difficult drudgery or boredom.

There is a Truly Amazing Life waiting for us right now...today! We can turn those feelings around almost instantly.

Remember Who You Are! Ask yourself in the mirror, "What is most important to you?"

Then free yourself and let go of what your ego wanted.

Be humble! So what if you've been working toward that thing you thought you wanted for the last 5 years and you're just now realizing it's not what your true self wanted all!

Are you going to throw away the next 5 years and miserably slog along the same way? Of course not!

Be true to You no matter how hard, or uncomfortable, or how much change that will require.

Listen to the real You today!

When you're breathing deeply and looking in your eyes, reminding yourself of your true nature and your compassionate loving spirit, spend some time asking what you really want and why.

Then listen.

Be still.

Don't be in a hurry.

Feel free to let the answers wait if they're not immediately forthcoming. Come back and ask again in the evening, or the next day.

And say, "I love you!"

It's a beautiful lifelong process of deepening your relationship with You. Enjoy it and savor every moment of it. There's no rush.

Make today amazing!

Day 25 - Cherish each precious quiet moment you have with yourself!

Can you believe how fast four weeks have flown by?

Speaking of believing, I've brought in Norman Vincent Peale, one of my favorite people ever, to share a bit on that today, but first...

I hope these exercises and lessons this month have been highly valuable to you.

Please feel open about sharing your experiences, positive or negative with me, or with the TAL Family.

My chief aim is to help you live a Truly Amazing Life. So I am open to anything I can learn about you so I can learn and become better. And I have no problem hearing about things that could be improved.

So please share!

Now, let's hear what Norman has for us:

"*Believe in yourself! Have faith in your abilities!* **Without a humble but reasonable confidence in your own powers**

you cannot be successful or happy." - Norman Vincent Peale

Yes! So true. Life is so much harder when you don't believe in yourself.

Maxwell Maltz in *Psycho-cybernetics* wrote:

"Low self-esteem is like driving through life with your hand-brake on."

Ever tried to ride a bike with the brakes dragging? It's the same feeling my friend Katie McCarthy spoke of two days ago when her work just felt so grindingly hard.

The reason it felt so hard was because she had lost her self-confidence.

How can you believe in yourself and have a high self-esteem if you don't even *Remember Who You Are?*

This habit of focused connection time in the mirror every morning and night will give you those by-products. You will gain confidence, belief, and higher self-esteem.

You are releasing the brakes from your ride through life each time you *Remember Who You Are.*

You are free to drive the speed life wants to take you, which is exhilarating.

Are you still doing the mirror technique daily?

Keep it up!

Have you felt sometimes you are just going through the motions?

If so, I can totally relate. After years of doing it personally, I've noticed times when I'm slipping into a hollow routine.

But I don't let it last long. Usually not even a day, because my connection time is just too precious to me.

How do we get out of those empty ruts though?

Just change it up a bit!

Follow your heart! Ask yourself new questions. Be playful and loving with yourself.

When you only go through the motions you miss out on the emotion. You may miss the joy of connecting with your true Self every single day, multiple times.

The goal of this habit is to stay connected to your true Self all throughout the day...

...But it starts with one moment.

You now have the habit of checking in daily in the mirror. Make sure to maximize that habit by slowing down for the moment and really being there for yourself.

Going through the motions just to check it off a list and move on is kind of like going out on a dinner date and checking emails on your phone the whole time. Hello? Anybody home? It's like the present moment isn't good enough or something...

...Remember to slow down!

Cherish each precious quiet moment you have with yourself! Even if it's brief.

You'll see yourself cherishing the time with your loved ones more too incidentally. You'll live more and more in the present and have less and less need to escape.

Now here's a beautiful thought to wrap up today from Claude Bristol in *The Magic Of Thinking Big*:

"<u>Every person is the creation of himself</u>, the image of his own thinking and believing. **<u>As individuals think and believe, so they are</u>**."

We are exercising our *believing* muscles of love here in this habit. We are consciously *thinking* the truth that we are loved, cared for, taken care of, and worthy.

And by continuously *thinking* that, and *believing* it daily, that becomes our reality. Our life is created beautifully out of that.

Make today amazing!

Day 26 - "Our self-image and our habits tend to go together."

Amazing morning to you!! Glad you are here! I love you!

Here is some more powerful wisdom from Maxwell Maltz to guide the discussion today:

"Our self image, strongly held, essentially determines what we become. **Our self-image and our habits tend to go together.** *Change one and you will automatically change the other."* - Maxwell Maltz

This one is really fascinating and is why this habit we are working on is like a double, or triple, or infinite whammy!

We are establishing the habit of high self-esteem!

This habit will literally snowball and spread out and drastically affect every area of our life.

By establishing this high image of ourselves, meaning we are deeply connected with our *TRUE* self, **all other** negative habits tend to just slip away over time *without a huge struggle.*

More from Maxwell:

"Realizing that our actions, feelings and behavior are the result of our own images and beliefs gives us the level that psychology has always needed for changing personality."

*"**Self-image sets the boundaries of individual accomplishment**."*

"The 'self-image' is the key to human personality and human behavior. Change the self-image and you change the personality and the behavior." - Maxwell Maltz

That is yet another reason why remembering who you truly are makes such a *HUMONGOUS* difference in your life.

When you *Remember Who You Are* you change your self-image.

You remember that you are truly amazing!

You remember that you are powerful!

You remember that you are beautiful, loving, compassionate, kind, smart, and infinitely capable!

You remember that you are connected to the source of all creation and you are a part of that creation, endowed with its power.

For me, that is embodied in this belief and remembrance: *I am a child of God.*

We tend to forget who we truly are, and so our self-image — or the picture we believe ourselves to be — fades into one of unworthiness, smallness, incapability, and weakness.

If those are the images we see inside, we have forgotten who we are.

Only in that state of forgetfulness do we struggle against negative habits, escape mechanisms, and addictions.

When we believe those lies of weakness and incapability to be true, then our actions are guided by falsehood.

I'm sure you've noticed those times when you <u>know logically</u> you don't want to do that thing that is harming you, <u>but for some reason you can't stop yourself!</u>

It's because subconsciously you were holding onto some lie about yourself that drove your behavior on autopilot.

But when we remember who we truly are we are free!

Then the negative patterns can fall away.

But what's the key to staying in this place of freedom?

THE KEY IS TO ALWAYS REMEMBER!

This habit we have created is the best way to ensure that.

Do whatever it takes to keep this habit forever.

Because as long as you Remember Who You Are, your self-image will be high, and you will be living a Truly Amazing Life.

Tomorrow we'll wrap up on this important topic, but for now...

...Make today amazing!

Day 27 - Life is magic when you truly believe in yourself.

Welcome to Today!! I love this day! Do you love being alive?

I hope so! I hope this message finds you in a place of love and compassion for yourself and all of life.

If not — if you are feeling oppressed and weighed down today by an onslaught of negativity or difficult circumstances — then my deep hope is that these words as reminders today will begin to lift your burden.

No matter what has happened, where you've been, what you've done in the past even as recent as one minute ago — *you can change your course RIGHT NOW and your emotional state can change.*

No state of feeling is permanent.

Remember that and see the beauty in the impermanence of life. It's always changing. You can always change your thinking for the better.

No matter what you perceive is going to happen in the future it can all be let go of, and you can choose to forget the past, smile at the future rather than worry about it, and be happy right now.

The easiest, fastest choice I'm aware of to make that happen, is the choice to go inward and *Remember Who You Are*.

Let's look at what the inspirational Bob Proctor has to say on this:

"We hold on to old ideas and old things, because we lack faith in our ability to obtain new ideas and new things. ***This of course, leads to a condition of insecurity, which stems, at its root, from an inability to understand who, and what, you are.*** *And a lack of awareness of your true relationship with the infinite power will always leave you with a distorted image of yourself."* - Bob Proctor, *You Were Born Rich*

So beautifully said.

Do you see how remembering who you truly are frees you from the past and future?

Knowing your true self, your true power, goodness, and capability, you no longer feel insecure about the future or a need to hold on to the past.

What happens when we don't remember, and we maintain a distorted image of ourselves?

<u>**WE SUFFER.**</u>

"Suffering is always the effect of wrong thought in some direction."

"It is an indication that the individual is out of harmony with himself, with the Law of his being. <u>The sole and supreme use of suffering is to purify, to burn out all that is useless and impure.</u>"

"**Suffering ceases for him who is pure**. There could be no object in burning gold after the dross had been removed, and a perfectly pure and enlightened being could not suffer." - James Allen, As A Man Thinketh

And how can you be pure?

Remember Who You Are.

Reject the false ideas of unworthiness and incapability and "I'm not as good as them" that press down from the world all around you.

Inside you are purity, goodness, and infinite capability.

Believing those truths eliminates the suffering caused by false beliefs and a distorted self-image.

<u>And then life is magic!</u>

"**Magic is believing in yourself. If you can do that, you can make anything happen.**" - Johann Wolfgang von Goethe

Belief is so vital to our happiness.

Lack of belief in ourselves is the main problem that develops when we forget who we are. If we don't remember our true nature, and we see ourselves as weak, of course we won't believe in ourselves!

Without belief life is pretty bleak.

We have no way to hold a high vision without belief. And "where there is no vision, the people perish."

"The vision that you glorify in your mind, the ideal that you enthrone in your heart, this you will build your life by, this you will become." - James Allen

And from Antoine de Saint-Exupery in *The Little Prince*

"<u>One sees clearly only with the heart. Anything essential is invisible to the eyes.</u>"

I love that statement so much!

I love the paradoxes of life, how much truth and wisdom they reveal.

We truly cannot see the essential with our eyes!

Strange huh?

But so true. Anything essential is invisible to the eyes and can only be seen clearly with the heart.

I hope you are seeing more clearly with your heart now after four weeks of daily practice.

Don't let this daily habit of remembering who you are fade.

Keep this habit as a permanent part of your daily life.

Stay connected to You!

This is among the most important things you can do for your life *for the rest of your life.*

And it's the most important thing you can do for others also, because only when you abide in the compassionate loving energy of your true Self can you give impactful and lasting service to others.

This is the last official lesson on this habit.

Next month we will move on toward mastery over one more of the 12 pillars of a Truly Amazing Life, as we stack together these habits of living amazingly.

Thank you for sticking with me faithfully for these four weeks! I'm proud of you and grateful to you.

As you go forth, continue to *Remember Who You Are!*

Be true to *You.*

And of course…

...*Make today amazing!*

Day 29 - Bonus Day! One more thought to wrap up.

I just couldn't resist giving you one last little nugget as you go forth to continue the habit to *Remember Who You Are* throughout your life:

"When we utilize the techniques of relinquishing the negative and surrendering resistance to the positive, sooner or later we come into a sudden, comprehensive awareness of our true dimension. Once this has been experienced, it will never be forgotten. The world will never intimidate us again as it once did." - David Hawkins.

I believe it is possible that the awareness of who we are can become so vivid and abiding that perhaps we don't need a ritualistic practice of remembering every day.

I certainly haven't arrived there though, and I think it's more common that we tend to forget if we don't have a ritual to remind ourselves…so let's keep the practice up!

I have found I definitely need a habit of reconnecting to myself daily or I tend to get disconnected from my inner self quickly.

But as soon as I remember who I am, the world does not intimidate me, and life is truly amazing.

How did it go this month building the habit to *Remember Who You Are*?

I'd be so grateful if you would take a moment and share your experiences from this past month with me and the TAL Family.

Let us celebrate your successes and breakthroughs with you!

Let us empathize with your challenges...tell us how we can help.

Please email me at aaron@trulyamazinglife.com with your thoughts on this month of habit training. I'd love to hear:

1. What worked well for you and what did you love?
2. On a scale of 1-10, how effective was this system in helping you find meaning and purpose, reclaim your passion for life, and unlock hidden treasures

of self-confidence & self-love? I'd love to hear about any breakthroughs you had.

3. Anything you think could be improved to make it more helpful for you?

Thank you so much for being a part of my life.

Thank you for giving me the opportunity to serve you!

Thank you for your desire to live fully and the loving energy and passion you contribute to the world.

All of this is a blessing to me.

And thanks in advance for sharing your feedback and experiences with me and with the TAL Family, it means a lot.

And as always...**make today amazing!!**

So What's Next?

You have now completed the training on habit #2 of the 12 Habits of a Truly Amazing Life.

I hope you have given it your heart and committed yourself to the simple practices for the full month.

That is how you will gain the most value in your life from this book. If you just so happened to opt for 'Way #2' of reading this book, and you read the whole thing in a day or two...now it's time for some self-discipline!

Make sure to be diligent about going back through each day *one at a time* and <u>take the actions over the course of an entire month!</u>

You will never know how impactful it could have been in your life if you don't.

Remember...living a Truly Amazing Life is a matter of habit. If you don't take the actions, you won't get the habits.

But when you do take the actions to establish or strengthen any one of the habits of a Truly Amazing Life® — life flows more smoothly.

It doesn't mean you won't experience hard things, but your ability to go through life with *poise* and *grace* dramatically improves.

Living the habits of a Truly Amazing Life® makes you like a wise sage — freed from the burdens of *attachment to pleasures* and *aversion to pain*. You can then embrace all that is and make the best of it in a state of peace and calm.

Having the 12 habits operating in your life is like building a house with power tools instead of slaving away with a handheld screwdriver and a handsaw.

You can do so much more, with greater ease and happiness, when you have these powerful habits installed.

I invite you to build on what you have started here and stay committed to living a Truly Amazing Life <u>by focusing on another habit next month</u>.

Here's a review of the 12 Habits & Pillars of a Truly Amazing Life ®:

	The Pillar	The Habit	The Book
1	Believe	Affirm	Affirm Your Truth
2	Remember	Reflect	Remember Who You Are
3	Smile	Appreciate	Smile! Feel Good Now
4	Enjoy	Move	Move Your Body
5	Think	Meditate	Think Better Thoughts
6	Succeed	Focus	Succeed Right Now
7	Give	Serve	Give Yourself Away
8	Create	Write	Create Your Life
9	Celebrate	Play	Play Every Day
10	Love	Forgive	Love Unconditionally
11	Grow	Read	Expand Your Mind
12	Empower	Listen	Empower Other People

The order you choose to focus on them is not critical. Pick whichever one jumps out at you or just go straight down the list.

Go to http://The12Habits.com to see all the books in the series that are currently available.

If, for example, you feel like you've been _struggling to move your body_ and you feel that's an area that could really improve your life — go next to the **Move Your Body** training.

I guarantee that training system will open your eyes and heart to new ways of looking at that important daily habit.

Or if you feel like you've had a hard time feeling deep joy despite all sorts of good things going on around you...start with **SMILE!** A focus on the essential habit of appreciation and gratitude will almost certainly turn that around.

All of the pillars are powerful and important.

You can't go wrong and you'll want to focus on one of the 12 habits each month anyway.

You'll get through each of them in one year taking one month at a time, so don't worry about what you may be missing. _Just make a decision and take action_.

If the decision is hard for you — just start at the top of the list.

Here are the two foundational posters once more in case you didn't yet take the opportunity to download and print them at the beginning of the month.

I highly encourage you to use these as daily visual reminders and motivators.

Positive words in your environment carry significant power.

The Make Today Amazing Poster - The 12 Habits

Go to http://TrulyAmazingLife.com/rwya-bonuses to download and print the poster for free.

The Truly Amazing Life Poster - The 12 Pillars

Go to http://TrulyAmazingLife.com/rwya-bonuses to download and print the poster for free.

What To Expect Going Forward

As you commit yourself to deepening these habits one per month at a time, here's what you can expect:

1 - **Simplicity** - By giving yourself only one focus per month you cut out the noise and distraction and allow for amazing growth and breakthroughs.

2 - **Consistent Growth** - Committing to strengthening one of the 12 habits of a Truly Amazing Life each month of the year will help you continue to grow and keep you from forgetting, getting swept away by life, and finding yourself lost or floundering.

3 - **Transformation** - As you systematically work on establishing one habit per month, you will look back after a year and witness remarkable change in yourself. You'll experience the wonderful benefits each month — but when you stack all of it together — it is inevitable that your life will feel incredibly rich, meaningful, and fulfilled.

That's the whole point after all...

...To live a Truly Amazing Life!

And that's what living these pillars and habits means. You literally cannot be living all 12 of these habits on a daily basis and NOT be experiencing a Truly Amazing Life.

That would be impossible.

So *trust the process* and *focus on these fundamentals* each day and each month.

In Closing

I will conclude with three huge THANK YOU's!

1 - *Thank you* for taking this training!

2 - *Thank you* for committing to yourself to constantly improve & grow.

3 - *Thank you* for your desire to live a Truly Amazing Life — the world is better because of your love.

I am truly honored that you have joined me in the commitment to never settle for mediocre ever again.

I love hearing about your experiences, *both successes and challenges.* I read every email personally at aaron@trulyamazinglife.com — please don't be shy about reaching out!

If we ever meet in person, I hope to give you a big hug and thank you in person for being the beautiful soul you are. That's how I see you in my mind, and in my heart.

I know that's who you are. I truly hope now at the end of this month together that you remember how *truly amazing* you are. I hope you are experiencing the joy in your relationship with yourself each day. Keep it up!

I love you. <u>Make today amazing!</u>

~ Aaron Kennard

How You Can Help!

Thank you again for taking this self-guided training course!

I really appreciate and need your feedback and input. It helps me improve and make things better for you in the future.

Please leave me a helpful review by going to http://TrulyAmazingLife.com/rwya-reviews

Reviews go a LONG way in helping spread this life-changing work to other people who could really benefit from it.

Thank you so much!

~ Aaron Kennard

www.ingramcontent.com/pod-product-compliance
Lightning Source LLC
Chambersburg PA
CBHW021149080526
44588CB00008B/273